Praise for

Wrestling with Wonder

"Marlo Schalesky's *Wrestling With Wonder* is one of the most important books I've read recently. Not one to tiptoe around life's thornier paths, she meets pain and trials head-on, within the context of Mary's life, according to sound biblical teaching. Insights and encouragement abound as Marlo delivers new perspectives on old old stories, making them relevant to our lives today. This is a major contribution to the literature on the human condition, worthy of a place next to C. S. Lewis's *The Problem of Pain*."

— **Dr. Rebecca Price Janney,** theologically trained historian and author of 18 books, including *Great Women in American History* and *Then Comes Marriage? A Cultural History of the American Family*

"This raw and achingly honest account speaks deeply to the doubts, fears, and discontent that keep so many believers from experiencing the true wonder of God's desire for us. Never is it promised that there will not be a cross where we will weep, where our hearts will be pierced, where we will hold death in our arms and not know the resurrection is coming. Yet in being chosen, like Mary, we have an all-encompassing solace, hope, and joy on this journey toward eternal life in the presence of Christ's glory."

— **Kristen Heitzmann,** bestselling author of Christy Award-winning novels *The Breath of Dawn* and *Secrets* and finalists *Indivisible* and *The Tender Vine*

"I started underlining as I read, then realized I was underlining practically every sentence on the page. So real. So raw. So identifiable. I found myself in the midst of Marlo's words so many times, and I ached as she shared not only her own journey, but Mary's wrestle with Wonder with such painful poignancy. Forever changed by this journey, I find my soul ultimately, blessedly soothed and drawn ever closer to the perplexing, amazing, and beautiful Christ."

—**Tamera Alexander,** *USA Today* bestselling author
of *To Whisper Her Name* and *A Beauty So Rare*

"Out of all the voice of truth and heart-wisdom out there, one author who I turn to time and again is Marlo Schalesky. *Wrestling with Wonder* guides our questions of "what if God doesn't love me" toward an understanding of who God is—in all His goodness and love—even in the face of life's hardships. My heart is full as I discovered within these pages who I am in God's eyes—highly favored, just like Mary. This is a book full of heart-transforming truths. Highly recommended!"

—**Tricia Goyer,** *USA Today* bestselling author of forty
books, including *The One Year Book of Amish Peace*

"*Wrestling with Wonder.* In a sense, it's something every Christian must do in order to know God in all His mysterious beauty. Exquisitely written, this book takes us by the hand and leads us to Bethlehem. To a place where Jesus can be birthed afresh and anew in each one of us."

—**Joanna Weaver,** author of *Having a Mary Heart*
in a Martha World

Wrestling

with

Wonder

Wrestling

with

Wonder

*A Transformational
Journey through the
Life of Mary*

MARLO SCHALESKY

ZONDERVAN

Wrestling with Wonder
Copyright © 2014 by Marlo Schalesky

This title is also available as a Zondervan ebook. Visit www.zondervan.com/ebooks.

Requests for information should be addressed to:

Zondervan, 3900 *Sparks Dr. SE, Grand Rapids, Michigan 49546*

Library of Congress Cataloging-in-Publication Data

Schalesky, Marlo M., 1967 –
    Wrestling with wonder : a transformational journey through the life of Mary /
Marlo Schalesky. — 1st [edition].
        p. cm.
    Includes bibliographical references.
    ISBN 978-0-310-33740-9 (softcover)
    1. Mary, Blessed Virgin, Saint – Meditations. 2. Mary, Blessed Virgin, Saint –
Biography. I. Title.
    BT608.5.S33 2014
    232.91 – dc23   2014011393

Cover design: Tobias' Outerwear for Books
Cover photography: Arcangel Images Inc
Interiorphotography: iStockphoto®
Interior design: Beth Shagene

First Printing August 2014 / Printed in the United States of America

To Jordyn,
who fills my life with wonder
and unexpected joy

Contents

Acknowledgments

There are always so many people that give of their time and hearts to make a book come to life. Here are just a few who helped make *Wrestling with Wonder* a reality, and a joy for me to write:

Thanks to Bryan Schalesky, my wonderful husband, first reader, and partner on the journey. You are, as always, God's special gift to me. Thank you for making this book possible. I appreciate how you've walked with me every step of the way.

Thanks to my kids, for letting me share your parts of my story, so that God may be revealed even in the hardest parts of life.

Thanks to my pastor, Mark Simmons, for access to your vast and extremely helpful library of books and commentaries. I couldn't have done it without your generous lending!

Thanks to my editors — Lori, Sandy, Laura, and Jim — for your helpful suggestions, insights, and encouragement. I so appreciate you all!

And thanks to the fine folks at Zondervan for catching the vision, believing in me, and taking a chance to make this book a reality. I thank God for you.

Bible Versions

Scripture quotations marked KJV are taken from the King James Version of the Bible.

Scripture quotations marked NASB are taken from the *New American Standard Bible*. Copyright © 1960, 1962, 1963, 1968, 1971, 1972, 1973, 1975, 1977, 1995 by The Lockman Foundation. Used by permission.

Scripture quotations marked NLT are taken from the *Holy Bible, New Living Translation*, copyright © 1996, 2004. Used by permission of Tyndale House Publishers, Inc., Wheaton, Illinois. All rights reserved.

Scripture quotations marked RSV are taken from the *Revised Standard Version of the Bible*, copyright © 1946, 1952, 1971 by the Division of Christian Education of the National Council of Churches of Christ in the USA. Used by permission.

Introduction

I *am Esau. Unloved. Unchosen.*
I am Cain. Rejected. Cast away.

I hear the words, unspoken, slithering through my soul. Esau, the older twin, favored by his father but unfavored by God. The one who would not receive the promise that had come through Abraham, his grandfather, and Isaac, his father. "Jacob I loved," said God, "but Esau I hated." Am I Esau?

Cain, who brought an offering to the God he worshiped only to have it rejected. Cain, confused, hurt, and angry because God said no. So jealous he killed his brother. Am I Cain? An outcast?

My palms press into the cold tile of the laundry room floor. Harsh, unyielding, the sound of my pain is lost in the steady thumping of the dryer, the slosh of cleansing clothes, and the wicked whisper of words that, for the moment, I believe.

It is dark here, gray, and far too ordinary for the doubts that roll through my mind. I shiver and savor them, tasting their bitterness. And I wonder, *Are they true? Do they define me?*

Esau. Cain.

Who am I? God, who am I to you?

I hear no answer except for the swish of soapy water and rhythmic thud of clothes that will soon be dry, fresh, ready to wear.

What am I doing here, a broken mess on the laundry room floor? To my shame, it isn't even tragedy that has driven me to my knees. It's not my twenty years of infertility. Of discovering that despite all my prayers, all my hopes, all the long and painful procedures, I am not pregnant again. I've been there. But not today.

It's not my six miscarriages. Not hoping beyond hope, cradling a belly that's supposed to hold new life, and losing. Again. I've been there too. But not today.

It's not a dead father, a difficult childhood, a death, a divorce in the family. Those have brought me to my knees, made me wrestle, made me weep. But not today.

Today it's nothing, really. And it's everything. It's a hundred little things piled up on a day when my husband is away on business, my baby just threw up, my toddler is crying, and I received another rejection — a small one, telling me I was unchosen. Unwanted. Passed by.

I should be fine. I should be happy anyway. After all, life is good. It's good enough. But I'm not fine. And I'm not happy. Instead, I am on the floor listening to the thump and slosh and crying out to a God who I'm sure doesn't care. And all the pain is back again. Of miscarriage and infertility, of death and disappointment. I feel it all again, and I am undone.

Why? Why am I a ragged mess, a broken child? Why am I a woman weeping on the floor when I'm supposed to be writing a talk on the wonder of God's immeasurable love? When I'm supposed to know, supposed to believe, supposed to no longer doubt? But I do doubt. And wrestle. Again. Still.

Who am I? Who is this God I say I believe, I say I trust?

Slosh. I hear the sound. And in it, a whisper. Less than a whisper. Only a wisp. *It is not easy to become clean. You must be tossed, spun. Beaten.*

Thump. It is a long process. Hot. Harsh. Unyielding.

And I see. I understand. A bit. A glimpse. A tiny glimmer of who I am. Who God is.

I shudder and push myself up from the hard tile. Cold on my

fingertips. Chilling. *God?* I watch the clothes tumble and spin. I watch. And breathe.

Then I glance left, to the changing table. The place where baby often squirms and shouts, cries and struggles as I work to make her clean. The place where she has grown from a tiny bundle that knew me only as a blur and scent to an almost-toddler who can hear the whisper of my voice from the other room and know that Mommy is near.

I step closer and run my hand over the terrycloth surface. I love her. But when she lies here, she doesn't understand. She knows she doesn't want to be here; she wants to get down and play. But I make her stay. I hold her still. I clean her. I do it because she is my loved one, my daughter, my favored child. But she doesn't understand my love.

I don't understand his. But the glimmer widens.

Perhaps I am not Esau. I am not Cain. Instead, I am like another woman who knelt in the darkness waiting to be cleansed. A woman who wept and did not understand. A woman whom God called "highly favored" and yet who found herself at a cross, with all her dreams crushed, all her beliefs challenged.

Did she kneel and weep and wrestle as I do? Did she pound her fists as the sky turned black as pitch? Did she ask my questions as all hope died? Who is this God of promise and pain who speaks of greatness, then comes as a babe in a feeding trough? Who is he whose declaration of favor leads him to a cross? Who is he when life goes awry and nothing goes as planned? Why is he not who I expected him to be?

And that's when I see it. I am Mary. The favored one. Not the beautiful little figurine in my Precious Moments nativity set. Not the peaceful-looking statue holding the form of a baby in my childhood church. But the woman for whom God's favor looked like a stable, like rejection, like kneeling at the foot of that blood-stained cross.

This is a love I hadn't thought to look for. A love that defies my expectations that God's favor should mean success, comfort, and prayer answered according to my wants. It should mean that life will go well and smoothly. But then I would never become who he meant me to be.

After all, everyone wants to be highly favored by God. And yet everyone faces hardships, life's unexpected twists and turns, and times when God seems absent. What do we do with this apparent discrepancy? Doesn't God's favor mean that he'll do what we ask, grant us success, and make our way through life smooth and joyful? Not for Mary. Not for me. Not for any of us.

So the questions change from the slithering hiss of "What if he doesn't love me?" to an awed whisper — "What if?"

What if God's blessings don't look like good health, secure finances, and fulfilling relationships? What if his favor includes pain, poverty, sorrow, and even death? What if it's about a hundred little things that seem to go wrong? What if favor is found through shattered dreams and on cold tile floors? That was Mary's life. And it is mine.

What if…

I am not Esau.

I am not Cain.

I am Mary.

And God is more passionate, wilder, and more wondrous than I ever believed him to be. What if he is calling me, and you, deeper than our own dreams? What if he's calling us to the foot of the cross?

Come, walk with me on this journey of God's favor. Discover your own journey in Mary's. Come as we turn the camera angle outward to focus not on Mary's attributes, character, or personal qualities but instead on the character and qualities of the God who burst into her life and changed everything. Come as we ask not, "Who is Mary?" but rather "Who is this amazing, perplexing God who reveals himself in new and startling ways through Mary's journey?"

Through this contemplative, transformational study of the life of Mary, you are invited to see God's purpose, discover how he works in the lives of those he calls "highly favored," and encounter him in deeper and more relevant ways. You are invited to be confronted and changed by this love that is not based on securing your happiness but on God's commitment to making you into the person he created you to be.

So, come and discover the unexpected Christ. Wrestle with wonder. And find him where you never expected him to be. Find him on the wild journey from an angel's unexpected arrival to beyond an empty tomb.

Come, if you dare ...

CHAPTER 1

Unexpected Interruptions
The Angel's Arrival

LUKE 1:26 – 38

I approach Mary's life on tiptoe, trembling, because I know I am treading where angels have trod—and where the church has stomped around for millennia. She has been revered, scorned, and sometimes even deified. And yet was she really so different from you, from me? Didn't she have similar hopes, similar dreams? A home of her own, a family, maybe even a dog. She was just a young girl from the backwoods of Galilee. A girl with a plan and a heart.

A good plan.

A good heart.

Yet the two could not exist together.

Like you, like me, Mary was called to more.

Because her God, our God, has dreams of his own, dreams that we can barely imagine. Like you, like me, Mary was called to more. Her God is our God. Her encounters with him more like our own than we might realize.

On one simple, ordinary day, her life was interrupted. Perhaps it happened like this ...

Mary Tells Her Story

I am Mary ... on an ordinary day in an ordinary life in an ordinary village tucked into the back corners of a region far from the hub of importance. I glance out the kitchen window. Swirls of dust rise and dance from the path outside. Just like every day. Blades of grass peek between cracks in stone. A bit of wild mustard blooms. And beyond that, an *akanthos* bush, its sharp thorns a symbol of our nation's shame.

The hem of my mother's dress disappears around the corner. She has gone to gather gossip near Nazareth's well. She'll be back soon enough, when the sun tips over the neighbor's rooftop. Meanwhile, I stand here, my fingers sunk deep in warm dough. I press and knead, massaging the flour and yeast, thinking about nothing, and everything. I think about the Romans and their oppression of my people. I think about promises made to Israel even before our nation was called from the loins of a single man. I think about the dough in my hands, the bitter herbs on the table behind me. My name means "bitter." But I am not my name. I am happy.

I see the neighbor's dog barking at a lone butterfly. He twirls and shakes his head. I laugh. Maybe I will have a dog when I have a home of my own. When the herbs are mine, the bread my own. My betrothed is out there somewhere even now, working on some table or doorway or cart. Working with strong hands and an honest heart. He is a descendant of the great King David himself. A *tsaddik*. It means "righteous." I am blessed to be betrothed to such a one. And before the year is up, I'll move from my parents' house to his. Then I will go to the well to gather gossip like beads on a string. I will sweep my own home, please my own husband, and bear children who will not be named for bitterness.

I roll the bread and pat it, warm beneath my hands. A rustling sound flutters the air behind me. I turn.

And see him.

A man but not a man. Like nothing I have ever seen before.

Breath squeezes from me. I cannot speak. Cannot even gasp.

He stands there in blazing white. Tall and strong. Shining. Extraordinary.

Terrifying.

And I know he is not a dream, not a vision. Somehow, he is real. And he is here.

The air stills, slows, shimmers around this one who is come from God.

In the silvery silence, he approaches me. He raises a hand.

Who are you? The question whispers through my mind, unspoken, chasing a hundred others that are swallowed in his glory. But I need no answer. I have heard of such things. Of such ones.

He is a messenger from God. *In Nazareth?*

He looks at me. Gently, fiercely, his eyes like fire in my soul. And he speaks.

"Be glad." A common word. Rejoice. An uncommon greeting. And from him, nothing is common at all. Then he says a word I don't understand. A word that speaks of extraordinary grace. He calls me "favored one." Me? Doesn't he know? I am an ordinary girl in an ordinary town on an ordinary day.

But not anymore.

"The Lord is with you."

And now I am trembling, troubled. What kind of greeting is this? What does he mean?

He says it again.

"Do not be afraid. You have found favor with God."

Favor? Grace? Here in the kitchen, in Nazareth, a barely betrothed girl with her hands full of dough?

He sees my confusion, my lingering fear. And he whispers, "Behold," the word for "see." But what he wants me to see is impossible. He tells me a story so wild, so crazy, that I don't know what to say, what to think.

He says, "Behold, you will conceive in the womb and will bear a son, and you will call the name of him Jesus. This one will be great, and he will be called the Son of the Most High, and the Lord God will give him the throne of David, his father. And he will rule over the house of Jacob into the ages, and of his kingdom there will not be an end!"

It is more than I can comprehend. More than I can see. So I focus on the one thing, the first thing. The impossible. "How will this be? I'm a virgin."

And then comes the wildest part of all. He doesn't speak of men. He speaks of miracles. He tells me the Holy Spirit himself will come upon me and God's power will overshadow me. Me! A simple girl from a backwater town filled with dirt and thistles and the occasional butterfly.

"Therefore, the child to be born will be called holy, the Son of God."

An incredible plan. An astounding promise. I cannot fathom that he speaks to me. Because it is more than a plan. More than a promise. It is a call. A question. Will I leave all my plans, all my hopes, behind me? Will I set my simple dreams aside? I will not have a dog. I may not ever sweep my own home, bake my own bread. Will I say yes to this shining messenger of God? Will I lay aside my ordinary life to embrace this vision of something new, something impossible, beyond anything I ever imagined?

He is talking again. About Elizabeth now. About the barren one having a son in her old age. We'd prayed for years, made whispered pleas at the temple. Elizabeth becoming a counterpoint to my call — the virgin giving birth alongside the barren one with child.

"Nothing is impossible with God."

Nothing.

Do I dare believe it? Do I dare say yes? I know what it means. Nothing will be the same again. No one will understand. How will anyone else believe? Can I bear the shame? Can I bear the disbelief? And more, can I bear the beauty? And the wonder?

And in this ordinary moment on an ordinary day in an ordinary life, I feel the heavens waiting, breathless.

Will I say yes?

"I am the Lord's servant." I exhale the words. I am his slave, his maidservant, his own creation. "May it be done to me according to what you've said." And so I accept. I surrender — not knowing what it means, these words I say, but knowing that I mean them. And knowing that YHWH himself hears.

My shining messenger smiles.

I tremble.

Then he is gone. And with him, everything I ever thought my life would be.

A Journey into Wildness and Wonder

That is how it is with this beyond-our-expectations, out-of-the-box God: we encounter him and nothing is ever the same again. He comes to us, he calls us to a new vision, a new way, a new dream. He breaks into our ordinary lives with a call to more than we can imagine.

And if we accept the call, if we choose to be his handmaiden, then nothing is the same again. Life becomes a crazy, wild ride with Jesus, who is not the tame, safe God that we expect him to be.

Just like Mary, my personal journey into wildness and wonder began with an interruption, a call, and a surrender.

An Interruption

I remember the day God first broke into my life, interrupting my ordinary with a glimpse of wonder beyond my wildest dreams.

That is how it is with this out-of-the-box God: we encounter him and nothing is ever the same again.

For me it happened in a dorm room at Stanford University. I lay on my rumpled bed with chemistry books scattered among great works of Western culture. A thin tome by Bernard of Clairvaux, a fat text with selected works from Martin Luther, a black paperback of the *Confessions* of Augustine. Chemistry and *Confessions* and Clairvaux—and midterms the next day. I stared out the window and followed the dance of dead leaves over the brick walkway outside. I heard the rustle of them through the slightly opened pane. And then it came. An inaudible whisper. A flutter in my soul.

I love you.

God?

And then came the tiniest glimpse in my heart of a love like I'd never seen, never experienced before. Sweet and piercing. Like the quiet whisper of a relentless wind. Like the powerful pull of the ocean's tide. Like deep, rumbling laughter. Like thunder across the sky.

God loved me.

With a love that broke me. Restored me.

Called me to more.

To surrender.

So there, among books and papers and pencils chewed to a nub, I accepted the call of love. I gave my life to the one who loved me with *that* kind of love.

I am yours, God. May it be to me as you want …

I didn't speak those words exactly, but it was what I meant, an echo of a girl who had encountered God millennia before me.

And like her, I knew some of what it meant to say those words. For me it meant a new major (in chemistry, of all things!), digging deep into the Bible with friends, choosing worship over achievement. But, in truth, I had no idea what I was really getting myself into. I didn't see years of infertility, miscarriage, disappointments, and doubts. I didn't see failures in ministries, family and friends who didn't understand, confusion and darkness.

All I knew was that he loved me and I was his. And that changed everything. I'd been called. Called out of my ordinary life with my ordinary plans. Called to something more.

More wondrous? Yes. But also more painful, more confusing, more wild and unexpected than I ever could have imagined. Because that is what it means to follow him. It means your plans are no longer your own. Your life itself belongs to him.

> *To follow God means your plans are no longer your own. Your life itself belongs to him.*

A Call

Just like me, Mary had been interrupted by a call to more. And what a calling!

It began with an unexpected interruption in an ordinary, well-planned life. Scholars believe that when the angel appeared, Mary was twelve to fourteen years old, which was the traditional age for betrothed girls of the time. Once betrothed, a girl was considered legally (but not domestically) married. She lived in her father's house for about a year to prepare before being taken to her husband's home to begin a normal married life.

So there was Mary, a regular Jewish girl, betrothed, waiting for the rest of her life to begin. Waiting and planning and hoping. She was going to marry a carpenter, move to his house, raise a family in the out-of-the-way town of Nazareth, and be a good woman.

According to one commentator, "For all indicators, her life would not be extraordinary. She would marry humbly, give birth to numerous poor children, never travel farther than a few miles from home, and one day die like thousands of others before her—a nobody in a nothing town in the middle of nowhere."

But then came the call.

In that ordinary home to that ordinary life, a messenger appeared. God broke in with his glory.

And his first call was to joy! He began with the word *chairo*, which is not a common greeting. It is a word that means "rejoice, be glad, be filled with joy." It shares a root with the Greek word for grace.

The angel came not with a call to submit, to repent, or even with a call to duty but rather to rejoice in the interruption of God breaking in.

And that makes me want to dance. Because I believe that God comes to each of us and his first call is to joy. Think of what that means. He comes to you, to me, in the ordinary places of life. In the kitchens and laundry rooms, in the workrooms and classrooms, in the living rooms and offices and cars and shopping aisles. And he doesn't say, "You must, you should have, you didn't, you did, you-you-you." Instead, he whispers of joy, wooing us with a grace we don't deserve. Joy becomes his common uncommon greeting to us as well. To receive his call, to see and be glad. But the only way we can do that is if we are holding our own plans loosely. We cannot approach our lives, our days, or even our moments with a tight-fisted grip on what we think ought to be. We must rejoice in the interruptions. We must let go of our self-focus so we can receive his joy. That is our first call.

But where do we find this uncommon joy?

The angel Gabriel pointed to two places:

- God's favor
- God's presence

He said, "Rejoice, the one having been favored" (Luke 1:28, translation mine). Favored one. What does it mean? Is it more than "the one God likes for the moment" or "the one God has plucked out of the crowd ... for now"? Yes! But you can't see it in the English. To glimpse the wonder of God's promise here, we must take a look at the word in the original Greek, or more precisely, the tense of the word, because, you see, in the Greek the word for "favored one" is in the perfect tense.

I love the perfect tense, because when the New Testament writers use it, God has given us something deeper, something more we can discover by looking at the original text. In the Greek, the perfect tense is used to indicate something that has been completed and perfected in the past — it's already done, finished, perfect, unchanging. But it's not over. Rather, in its perfected, completed state, it has effects that continue on in that same perfected state through eternity. The effects don't end or diminish or wear out. They are established forever. When Jesus said, "It is finished" (John 19:30), and gave up his spirit on the cross, he used this tense.

And that is something beautiful. Because it means that God's favor for Mary, and for us, doesn't depend on us. It has been perfectly established already, and we can live in it today, tomorrow, forever. It is finished, complete.

God's favor doesn't depend on us. It has been established already, and we can live in it today, tomorrow, forever.

That's not all. The word tense is also passive, again emphasizing that Mary has done nothing or will do nothing to earn God's favor. It has already been given freely to her by his grace. She wasn't favored because she was super-spiritual or extra-holy or ultra-faithful. "Indeed, she is not introduced in any way that would recommend her to us as particularly noteworthy or deserving of divine favor," says commentator Joel Green. She was just a virgin betrothed to a guy named Joseph. But she was favored, graced. Why?

Gabriel gave the reason immediately: "The Lord is with you" (Luke 1:28). He is with you too.

Ponder that for a moment. Soak in an understanding of favor, of grace, that is based on God and his presence, not on us and our doings. Not on our accomplishments, our possessions, our positions, our successes, or even our work in his kingdom. That's what God offers us: a call to grace and joy, a statement of who we are in God (his favored one), and a reminder of his presence.

We are ordinary. He makes us extraordinary. Because of grace. Because of his presence with us.

The angel came not with a normal, traditional greeting but rather with one that confounded even early church theologians. Origen, from the late second and early third century, wrote, "The angel greeted Mary with a new address, which I could not find anywhere else in Scripture!" The greeting doesn't say "hello" but rather announces the wondrous presence of God himself. And that's what God's favor is all about. You don't walk alone. Not through the difficulties, not through the blessings, not even through the ordinary moments that may seem devoid of anything that matters. It *all* matters now, because God is with you. Always. In every moment. With his favor.

Yet, for Mary, and so often for us, this is a very perplexing greeting, a very strange call. It is both wondrous and scary. Wondrous because God has broken into the ordinary and made it extraordinary. Scary because it means Mary's plans, and our plans, don't matter anymore.

Then came the second call in Mary's life, and in ours: "Fear not!" Don't let fear stop you; don't let it be your response to God. Don't turn away and hide! Why? Because, again, you have found not judgment, not condemnation, not indifference but favor from God.

So, what is this favor really? What does God's presence with us mean? For Mary, and often for us, it means a new dream, a new plan, a new life. One that we may not understand yet. One that may seem strange and impossible, that will promise discomfort as much as success. One that will most likely upend our lives!

But that's what God's favor, what his dynamic presence, really means. It means a call out of the ordinary into the extraordinary. It means the Savior himself comes into our lives.

To Mary, it must have seemed crazy. R. Kent Hughes explains it this way: "She understood the gist of the angel's announcement: 'You are going to become *pregnant*; you are going to call your son's name *Salvation*, he is going to be the *Son of God*; and he will be *the Messiah*.' What an earful! What an incredible heartful!"

God's plans for us may seem crazy too. It may seem that what he calls us to is impossible. So, like Mary, we may ask, "How will this be?" Not "Will this really be?" Rather, "*How* will it be?" How will God accomplish his purposes in our lives?

He answers us the same way he answered Mary: by the Holy Spirit. Gabriel said, "The Holy Spirit will come on you, and the power of the Most High will overshadow you" (v. 35). You see, there's something mysterious, something beyond us, in this call to be his. There's something about his overshadowing power that makes the impossible more than possible. And that makes the results holy. Gabriel said, "The one being born will be called holy" (v. 35, translation mine). What is born from the Holy Spirit, from God's power in our lives, is holy.

The life that comes when we receive God's call is no longer ordinary. Instead, that life is holy. Your everyday, in-and-out, kitchen life is holy.

That's what it means to follow God — to open your life to the unexpected Christ. It means encountering him in the ordinary and finding that life has become extraordinary. It means the impossible thing is real. It means taking a step into wonder … because life is now holy.

But how can we know it's true? How can we trust? We just have to look around. Gabriel pointed to Mary's relative, Elizabeth, once barren and now pregnant. "See," he implied, "God has done the impossible before. He's doing it now in the life of someone close to you."

It is the same for us. Look around you. See the lives of people he's changed. See the footprints of God's power in places where hope seemed dead.

> *To follow God means encountering him in the ordinary and finding life extraordinary. It means the impossible thing is real.*

And see them in all God has done in the past as well. "For no word from God will ever fail," Gabriel said (v. 37), echoing the words of the angel to Abraham and Sarah in Genesis 18:14: "Is anything too hard for the LORD?" God kept his promise to a long-barren couple and the nation of Israel was born. He will keep his promise to Mary as well. And to you. And me.

And Christ will be born in our lives, in our circumstances, in our everyday encounters. Because Gabriel literally said, "For *every word* will not be impossible with God." That means everything God says, everything he plans, everything he dreams, is now possible. Even a nation being born from a barren woman. Even a young virgin from a backwoods, out-of-the-way village in Galilee giving birth to the Savior of the world. Even God transforming your everyday, sometimes boring, sometimes messed-up, sometimes confusing and frustrating and doubting and imperfect life into something amazing for his glory.

God revealed himself to Mary, and he has also revealed himself to us. He is the God of the impossible; he always has been. He is the God who called us to joy, to abandon fear, to release our dreams to embrace his.

A Surrender

So what will be our answer? Mary's was a resounding, "Yes!" "I am the Lord's slave," she said. "May it be done to me according to your word" (v. 38, translation mine). She proclaimed herself fully belonging to God—his slave, his servant, his handmaiden, one with no rights of her own, no separate life, no eight-to-five job with the rest of her time being her own. She chose to be a person who fully, wholly, belonged to her Master.

She surrendered. And she didn't need great understanding, or to have everything all figured out, or to see God's plan from beginning to end. She had no idea what her surrender would really mean. She didn't know it would lead to a manger, to a cross. But she did know that God called her to lay down her dreams and plans in order to embrace his. And she knew there would be a cost.

After all, she was betrothed to Joseph. She must have expected him to react badly. Matthew tells that Joseph did think of divorcing her (Matt. 1:19). And even though the death penalty for adultery described in Deuteronomy 22:23–24 seems not to have been carried out often, she still could have been stoned. Mary knew that a "yes" would mean suffering and might even bring death. But she said it anyway. She let go of her grip on her own dreams and expectations of life. And she embraced God's instead.

Will you? Will I? Not just once. Not just in a kitchen or a church service, at camp or in a living room with friends. But every day. Every hour. Will we be willing to let go of our "Josephs," our houses on the knoll, our orderly lives and dreams and goals? Or will we cling to our own "house"—our own dreams of family, success, and how life ought to be? The call is to lay those aside and instead identify with God's household, be his slave, accept a new adventure, accept the favor of his presence. Rejoice.

Rejoice?

That our dreams are endangered? That we maybe won't get the life we planned for, the life we always wanted?

Rejoice?

Yes.

And surrender. Because you are highly favored. God is with you. And that changes everything.

Can you accept it?

Who Is This God?

But I accepted Christ years ago, you may say. What does this have to do with me?

Everything. Because I think God often breaks into our ordinary, everyday lives with a call to more. It may be in the kitchen, in the classroom, in the office, or even in the laundry room. And there he is, interrupting our lives with a greater vision, a deeper call. Wooing us to wonder with an impossible dream. With his dream, not ours. Because *he* is with us.

"Be somebody!" says the world. "Be mine," says God. "Stop striving and instead rest in my plans for you."

So, we must ask, who is this God? Who is he who interrupts our lives with a call to the impossible?

He is the dream taker and the dream maker.

The Dream Taker

"Follow your dreams!" says the world.

"Die to self," says God. "Die to your plans, your dreams, your tightfisted grip on what your life should be."

"You can do anything you set your mind to!" says the world.

"I am God; you are not," says God. "Submit to me, and together we will do everything *I* set *my* mind to."

"Be somebody!" says the world. "Accomplish, achieve, fight your way to the top!"

"Be mine," says God. "Stop striving and instead rest in my plans for you. Will you be my handmaiden?"

The Dream Maker

Meditate on these verses. Hear in them God's call to you:

- "Take delight in the LORD, and he will give you the desires of your heart" (Ps. 37:4). Not "Take delight in the Lord and he will do whatever you want." Instead, he will give you the desires themselves—new desires, new dreams, *his* dreams for you. His dreams will become yours!

- "For we are God's masterpiece, created in Christ Jesus for good works, which God has already prepared for us to walk around in" (Eph. 2:10, translation mine). He has already favored us with a plan and a call. It's all prepared. We just have to let go and step forward.

- "'*I* know the plans *I* have for you,' declares the LORD" (Jer. 29:11, emphasis mine). And they aren't our plans. They aren't our dreams. They aren't our carefully scripted ideas for what our lives should be. Instead, they are a call to the impossible—to loss, confusion, difficulty, misunderstandings, ridicule—and ultimately to wonder.

So in the great calls and in the small: rejoice, fear not, and submit. Whisper to God, "Let it be to me as you have said."

Do you dare? Mary did. And so the adventure began—an adventure that would look nothing like her expectations. She would enter a life that at every turn seemed to go awry, where nothing would make sense, where doubt and confusion, pain and fear were her companions, where the Son of God himself would seem to have lost his mind.

But she would find him on the journey and become who she was always meant to be.

What about me? What about you?

Do you long for your own wild and wondrous adventure with

an unexpected God who does the impossible in ways you never imagined? If so, let go! Open your white-knuckled fingers wrapped around your ordinary plans. Accept the wild, crazy gift of a call that will defy all your expectations. Because once you say yes, you will embark on a journey where nothing is as it seems, nothing happens as expected. A journey that will lead to the foot of a cross.

     So rejoice,

    fear not,

   submit.

Do you dare?

      If so, turn the page and hang on.

CHAPTER 2

Blessedness Redefined
A Trip to the Hill Country

LUKE 1:39–56

W e surrender. We let go. We take the first step on this wild adventure that God has for each of us. We begin the journey. Truth fills our lives, washes over us, gives us a vision beyond our dreams. We are filled with a new hope of what life will be.

We are blessed.

And we sing.

Because God is changing everything. He is turning our world upside down. And what we think we know, we don't. What we've been taught is "the way it is," isn't. What we've believed couldn't be altered becomes like a fleeing mist.

Hope and beauty and wonder collide in this new world where blessedness flows over us. But what is this blessedness? What is it really? A feeling? A vision? A hope? Or is it something else, something more?

Could it be that God is turning our idea of blessedness upside down too?

> *Could it be that God is turning our idea of blessedness upside down?*

Could it be that blessing is something beyond what we ever dreamed?

I wrestle with this new idea of blessedness as I consider the hopes that must have soared through Mary's heart after the angel left her. What did she think? What did she believe? What did blessedness mean to her in those first steps of her wild journey?

How did the truth of the coming Messiah resonate in her soul? How does it resonate in ours?

What happened next? Perhaps it went something like this ...

Mary Tells Her Story

Blessed. The word whispers through my mind as I make my three-day journey to Elizabeth's house. A four-day journey, but it will take me three because I hurry. I must see Elizabeth. I must behold the truth of her promise-come-true, see her belly round with child, and share her joy. I must know that God's blessings are for more than just me.

Blessed. It defines me now. A strange word. A strange concept. To know that the Promised One, the one we have waited for, grows in me. My belly is still flat. No outward sign shows his presence. But I know he is there. My Messiah, the Long-Expected One. My son. And God's.

I shiver. Grip my garments in hope. And I run. Even though I am expecting. Perhaps because I am expecting. More than a baby. More than a king. I am expecting the world to be right again and all things to be made new. Every promise fulfilled. A new world for me, for my people.

Dust billows around me, squeezes into my sandals, settles in the folds of my tunic. As a woman betrothed, I should be secluded in my father's house. But I am not. What the angel told me has changed everything. It has changed me. So I run.

I walk. I leave everything behind me, including a husband whom everyone will know is not the father of the child I bear. But I go where I must.

I go toward Jerusalem. And I wonder: *Is this a journey my son will also take? Will he approach Jerusalem, where all the old promises will come true? Will he enter that great city of old, the city of prophets, and be the Messiah they foretold?*

I know he will. And so I hurry. In the direction of Jerusalem. To my cousin. Who holds her own miracle. Will she rejoice with me? Will she understand this strange thing that has happened to us both?

Will she see that we are both blessed?

Then I see Zechariah's house tucked into the hill country of Judea. A modest home fit for a priest in the long line of Levi. *Will their son be a priest too?* I wonder. *Or will he be more?* My hand touches my belly. My son is still a secret. I won't tell her. Not yet.

My feet close the distance between the road and their home. I open the door and enter. I call out my greeting.

Elizabeth comes toward me. She grasps her round belly and gasps. Her eyes capture mine. Light shines from her face. And her smile warms my soul. She cries out, she shouts the one word that has echoed through my heart: "Blessed!"

"Blessed are you among women, and blessed is the fruit of your womb!" she cries.

I hesitate. How did she know? Could it be that the Spirit, God's Spirit, is here? Have the prophets returned, just as foretold? The prophet Joel told us that in the day of the Lord, our God would pour out his Spirit on his servants, on both men and women. And now the Spirit has come upon Elizabeth.

Her arms stretch toward me as more words tumble from

her lips. "And why has this happened to me — that the mother of my Lord should come to me?"

She knows that my baby is the Holy One. She speaks not of her own pregnancy, her own child, but of mine!

"For behold, when the sound of your greeting came to my ears, the baby in my womb leaped for joy!"

Even the baby knows. And he leaps for joy! An image comes to my mind, one of David leaping with joy before the ark of the covenant. I am the ark, the bearer of the promise, the one who holds the hope of Israel. I tremble. Who am I that I should be so blessed?

"And blessed is the one who has believed that there will be a fulfillment of the things spoken to her from the Lord."

Blessed. Yes, I am blessed. I am filled with hope. I am filled with joy.

And I remember the promises, I remember what we in Israel have hoped for. I remember Hannah who sang in her pregnancy so many years before me. I remember David's psalms and his son's proverbs. I remember Habakkuk and the promises of the prophets of what this child will be. I remember it all. This is what God has done for me, for us, through the baby I am expecting.

And so I sing:

> My soul magnifies the Lord,
> and my spirit rejoices in God my Savior.

For this moment, I know only joy, only hope. My heart swells with that hope, the vision of his salvation.

> For he looked upon the humble state of his servant,
> his bondslave.

He chose me. Me! Not a king's daughter. Not a ruler. Not a

grand and glorious woman of stature and influence. Just me, a simple girl from the country.

> For behold, from now on, all generations will consider
>   me blessed,
>   for the Mighty One did to me great things,
>   and holy is his name!

Blessed! Because of this baby. He has done this. Not me. Him. And so the reversals begin. From my humble state to divine blessedness. The blessed one is not the one we would have expected. Instead, it is me. What other reversals will I see through this child I bear?

> And his mercy is to the ones fearing him
>   from generation to generation.

From the generations of Israel from of old, to now when the promise is fulfilled, to every generation to come. This child has changed everything. For me, for my people. For the world.

> He did a mighty deed with the arm of him.
>   He scattered the proud in the thoughts of their heart.
>   He brought down rulers from thrones
>   and lifted up the humble.

No more proud, arrogant men ruling over us. He has done it, just as he did in Egypt when he freed our people from four hundred years of slavery. With this baby, he has brought down the arrogant ones from their thrones. It is a new day for us, for all of God's people. It is the reversal we have been waiting for, when the high ones will be brought low and the low ones lifted high. We have waited so long.

> The hungering he filled with good things,
>   and the rich he sent away empty.

Another reversal. We who are so hungry for him, for his

righteousness, will be filled at last. We who have hungered both physically and spiritually will have our fill. But those who lorded over us, those who were rich at our expense, are sent away. We will be filled and free.

> *He helped Israel, his servant, to remember mercy,*
> *   just as he spoke to our fathers,*
> *to Abraham and his descendants forever.*

The world set right at last. Israel helped at last. All the promises of all the prophets fulfilled. Finally. What will this mean for my people? What will it mean for Rome? For Herod? What of our captors? Will we be a true nation again? Will we be God's chosen?

Will we be blessed?

I sing and am filled with the wonder of all the reversals, all the mercy, all the rightness that come with this Promised One.

For this moment, I see it all ... and I am blessed.

The Reversal of Blessedness

Blessed. Like Mary, I know that feeling of looking out on life and seeing it with new eyes. I know what it's like to sit on the mountaintop and sing because the beauty, the wonder, of what God will do is so amazing that I can barely contain the joy of it.

I know the blessing of getting a glimpse of God and having him be more beautiful than I dreamed.

And I know what it's like to sing like Mary and yet not realize that God is redefining what blessedness means to me.

I remember an afternoon in college just a few months after I'd surrendered my heart and life to Jesus. I biked out to a wooded hill miles from campus. There I hid my bike and hiked to the hilltop. I sat among the tall dry grasses and hovering oaks and looked out across a half dozen small valleys filled with trees and shadows. The breeze rustled through the grass and tickled the mustard blooms on the slope below me. Birds chirped, but no other sound came from the road far behind and below me.

I listened to the birds, to the breeze, to the shiver of oak leaves. I breathed in the scent of grass and wildflowers. I felt the warmth of the sun on my shoulders and the coolness of wind through my hair.

And there I thought and prayed and contemplated this God who had called me out of my old, ordinary life, into an extraordinary adventure with him.

I thought about God.

I thought about life.

I thought about how everything had changed.

Life was different.

Jesus lived in me.

And I was blessed.

So I sat there, my knees hugged to my chest, as God drew my attention to another far-off peak. And then I heard what was like another quiet whisper in my soul. *We are going there.*

From the tall hill I sat on to a taller mountaintop covered in gorgeous pine.

I held my breath then let it out slowly, because I knew God wasn't speaking of a literal trip to the mountain beyond me. He was showing me my life. My life was to be a journey from this hilltop to a distant mountain covered with beauty. And he would take me on this journey, walk beside me, guide me to the mountain far away.

I sang then. One worship song after another. I praised him, declared his glory, proclaimed my trust. Because I glimpsed the far-off mountain.

And I thought that's what it meant to be blessed.

But God was showing me something else. He was revealing to me not simply a mountaintop but a journey. And the path he would

> *Blessing is not so much the destination as the journey. It is walking in the shadows and finding God beside me.*

take me on would lead first through the dark valleys below me. It would wind through thick trees and dense underbrush. There would be times I couldn't see the sun. There would be moments I would believe I couldn't go on. I would trip and stumble in the darkness.

And for much of the journey, I wouldn't be able to see the mountaintop at all.

But he promised to walk with me. And he promised that the mountain was there, whether I could see it or not. He promised to take me there.

I thought blessedness was seeing the mountain.

He showed me that true blessedness is walking with him in the dark. Not a gentle stroll in the woods but a long hike beside my Savior.

So that day, I first glimpsed the idea that blessing is not so much the destination as the journey. It is not arriving at the perfect, beautiful place and settling down there. Instead, it is walking in the shadows and finding him beside me. And in that long journey, I would learn to see blessedness in a new way. I would discover what the word really means.

Mary would have to discover it too. And her first lesson happened in the hill country as Elizabeth declared her blessed and Mary sang her beautiful hymn of grace, of blessedness ... of reversals.

Blessed in the Hill Country

Mary hurried to Elizabeth's house shortly after her interaction with the angel Gabriel. We don't know why she went. To see if what the angel had said was true? To rejoice with her relative? To get away from pointed whispers or suspicious looks at home during the early stages of her pregnancy?

We don't know her motivation, but we do know that what she received was the confirmation of all her hopes, all her beliefs. Prudentius, from the fourth century, reflects on this passage through poetry:

> *Believe what says the angel who was sent*
> *From the Father's throne, or if your stolid ear*
> *Catch not the voice from heaven, be wise and hear*
> *The cry of aged woman, now with child.*
> *O wondrous faith! The babe in senile womb*
> *Greets through his mother's lips the Virgin's Son,*
> *Our Lord; the child unborn makes known the cry*
> *Of the Child bestowed on us, for speechless yet,*
> *He caused that mouth to herald Christ as God.*

Mary had her mountaintop experience as Elizabeth confirmed not only Mary's blessedness but also the significance of the baby she carried. Contemporary scholar R. Kent Hughes explains it this way: "How young Mary must have taken heart at old Elizabeth's shouts. Here was one who without any explanation immediately understood her secret and celebrated it by pronouncing a double blessing and affirming that Mary indeed carried the Lord and Messiah in her womb!"

Before this moment, Mary was alone in her journey. But now someone else knew the truth and embraced it. Someone she loved and respected confirmed God's promise and call. The coming Messiah was now more than just her own promise, more than a feeling inside. Mary received a taste of faith in community, of vision and confirmation outside of herself. And she was filled with hope, filled with joy.

She was declared blessed.

Blessed? Blessed!

But what would that blessedness mean? When Elizabeth proclaimed Mary as "blessed," she used a term that contains the word *logos* or *word* and, in Greek literature, had the connotation of speaking well of someone. We get the term *eulogy* from this word in the Greek.

To the ancient Hebrew, the word meant even more. Patriarchs spoke blessings over their children, God blessed his people, and Philo, a Hellenistic Jewish philosopher near the time of Jesus, used the word frequently in connection with receiving a reward. Mary, hearing the word from Elizabeth, may have thought of other women in Israel's history, such as Jael, who were specifically called blessed. In Deborah's song in Judges 5:24, Jael is proclaimed blessed for killing Sisera, the enemy commander of the Canaanite armies. For her, blessedness came through assassinating an enemy of Israel.

But God, through Mary, was doing something new. Blessed would not mean the conquering of a national enemy. It wouldn't mean reward or wealth. For Mary blessedness would look like a nearly one-hundred-mile trip while pregnant, an escape to Egypt because someone was trying to kill her child, a Messiah surrounded by Israel's rabble, and eventually kneeling at the foot of a Roman cross while her firstborn son died the most excruciating death known to the world. Her son, the Promised One, would be executed before her very eyes.

Blessed? Blessed! But not like Jael. She killed the enemy. Jael didn't see the enemy murder her beloved son. With Jael, we see the old view of blessedness, but with the coming of Christ, the word would mean something new, something more. For Mary and for us.

Breaking Old Paradigms

As in Mary's story, we often operate out of our old paradigms—out of old definitions of success, favor, and blessedness that we had before our surrender, before we gave up our dreams to embrace God's. We died to our own dreams but not to our hopes of what this life as God's maidservant will be. Like Mary, we need to discover that we are blessed but that blessedness means something different from our old way of thinking. Our ideas of success, victory, reward, and favor must be redefined. Instead, we must embrace the unexpected, upside-down answers to the promises he gives us.

Blessedness means something different from our old way of thinking. Our ideas of success, victory, reward, and favor must be redefined.

God is up to something greater than our hopes and beyond our wildest dreams. And while we can't know for certain what Mary thought her blessedness would mean, we might get a glimpse in the beautiful, soaring phrases, filled with faith, filled with hope, of what has come to be known as the Magnificat (a name derived from the first word in the Latin version of Mary's song). Laden with Old Testament images and promises, the Magnificat lays out Mary's vision of what the coming Messiah will mean not only to her but to her people.

Mary Sings

"The Magnificat ... marks the first human interpretation of the angelic annunciations. The angel simply announced what God was going to do. Humans are left to respond and to interpret it for others," says commentator David E. Garland. He then explains Mary's interpretation by saying, "Then she sings about what it means for Israel and all generations, depicting it as God's fulfillment of his promises in the present and as a great turnabout in circumstances of the mighty and the lowly (1:51–55)."

For Mary the coming of the promised Messiah meant that God had now done what he had promised through the Old Testament prophets. The song is filled with specific Old Testament allusions, motifs, and language. It recalls the depths and nuances of all the promises made to Israel from Abraham through the prophets. And now Mary used the past tense to show that in this baby she carried, all those promises had now, already, come true.

God had done it. The time had finally come. The promises were fulfilled. Mary saw the distant mountaintop. And she sang:

> *My soul magnifies the Lord,*
> *and my spirit rejoiced in God my Savior.*
> *For he looked upon the humble state of his servant, his bondslave.*
> *For behold, from now on, all generations will consider me blessed.*
> *For the Mighty One did to me great things,*
> *and holy is his name!* (vv. 46–49, translation mine)

Here again we see the word "blessed." But this time Mary used a different term in the Greek than the one Elizabeth used. Mary used *makarios*, the same word for blessed that we see in the Beatitudes of Matthew 5 and in Jesus' sermon in Luke 6. In Mary's time, the word would have been associated with good fortune, with those who had been blessed with happiness through family, material goods, fame, and other "good things" beyond those received by the normal person. It is significant that this is the very word Jesus would redefine in the Beatitudes. He would reverse the common meaning. According to Jesus, it was no longer the rich, the well-fed, the happy, and the well-loved who would be blessed, but the poor, hungry, weeping, and hated. It is this kind of reversal that characterizes the whole of Mary's song.

> *And his mercy is to the ones fearing him*
> *from generation to generation.*
> *He did a mighty deed with the arm of him.*
> *He scattered the proud in the thoughts of their heart.*
> *He brought down rulers from thrones*
> *and lifted up the humble.* (vv. 50–52, translation mine)

Mary looked across the dark valleys to see the mountaintop where mercy is coupled with might. Where the proud no longer rule over the faithful. Where the faithful are no longer subject to arrogant men on their thrones. She sang of a beautiful mountain where political power is reversed, where power itself is redefined to be the prerogative of the humble instead of the arrogant and proud. She saw the reversal of what it means to be powerful.

> *The hungering he filled with good things*
> *and the rich he sent away empty.* (v. 53, translation mine)

Rich and poor are redefined, reversed. The poor, the hungry, are filled. The rich are no longer rich but empty. With the coming of the Messiah, these words would no longer mean what they did before.

> *He helped Israel, his servant, to remember mercy,*
> *just as he spoke to our fathers,*
> *to Abraham and his descendants forever.* (vv. 54–55, translation mine)

Because Israel is God's servant, its role, its standing in the world, was reversed, not through the normal means of power but through God's amazing mercy.

And so Mary sang out of the Old Testament understanding of God's mercy and covenant (referenced in Ex. 2:24; 32:13; Deut. 9:27; 2 Sam. 22:51; Ps. 105:8–11, 42; and Mic. 7:20). She saw the promises to Israel alone, to Abraham and his descendants. She operated in the only paradigm she knew—the paradigm of an Old Testament Jew.

But God promised more. He promised that all the world would be blessed through Abraham's seed. He said, "Through your offspring all nations on earth will be blessed" (Gen. 22:18). And that was something new. Something beyond Mary's vision.

Israel's Messiah would come. And *all* the world would be blessed. Because God, through Jesus, would turn the whole world upside down. He would redefine everything. Even the definition of blessedness. Because he would not just bring about the reversal of poor and rich, hungry and filled. Jesus would be the reversal itself. He would be the Bread that fed the hungry. He would do more than provide it. He would *be* it. He would be the poor who is rich—the God brought down from his throne to become a human baby, the humble one who would be lifted up on a cross to die in order that all who put their trust in him might live.

This Messiah was not just the one who would bring about the fulfillment of the prophecies; *he* would be that fulfillment. He would be God born as a man, humility embodied, the Bread that filled the hungry, mercy not only for Israel but to the ends of the earth.

> *Blessedness is when all worldly paradigms are turned upside down and still we choose to sing.*

So Mary sang, she rejoiced, and in doing so, blessedness itself began to be redefined. The redefinition began with a song, a vision. It would lead through the valleys and shadows, between trees and through underbrush. It would be the blessedness of an incredible journey with a magnificent God.

Blessedness is when all worldly paradigms are turned upside down and still we choose to sing.

Who Is This God?

So who is this God who takes what we think we know and redefines it? Who is he who calls the poor rich, the hungry filled, the mighty fallen, the humble lifted high? Who is he who calls us blessed not when life has finally reached perfection but rather when we are struggling along on the journey?

This is the God of reversals.

This is the God of upside-down blessings.

This is the God who says:

> Blessed are you who are poor ...
> Blessed are you who hunger ...
> Blessed are you when you weep ...
> Blessed are you when people hate you ...
> Blessed are you when they exclude and insult you ...
> Blessed are you when you're rejected ...

This is the new blessedness—the reversal of all the world teaches, of all our culture says is the way things are supposed to be.

We think blessing is the arrival at the place where our troubles are gone and we are financially secure, well-fed, happy, liked, included, and spoken well of. Blessing is being accepted on the mountaintop.

But Mary shows us that through Jesus, God has changed everything. He has made the poor, hungry, weeping, hated, excluded, insulted, rejected people blessed. And he has done it by becoming poor, hungry, weeping, hated, excluded, insulted, and rejected.

Our world is turned upside down.

And it is on the journey through the shadows that God calls us to sing. It is there that he becomes more than the one who provides, but the Bread itself; more than the one who frees, but Freedom itself. More than a way out of darkness, but the Light.

Blessedness isn't a feeling or a synonym for happiness. It isn't having our lives conform to what we'd like them to be. Instead, blessedness is being chosen for a journey through deep valleys and scratchy underbrush. It's traveling with the one who changes everything and walks beside us in the dark. It's singing, knowing the reversals are coming, knowing our world is being turned upside down. It's supposed to be that way. We're on a journey to the mountaintop.

The only question is ...

Will we sing along the way?

CHAPTER 3

Rough Journeys

Pregnant, on a Donkey, Really?

LUKE 2:1–5

An almost one-hundred-mile journey. Pregnant. On a donkey. Or on foot. I turn the concept over in my mind, taste it, touch it. The dust, the stones, the pressure of a babe kicking against a womb too tight for such travels. I don't want to imagine it. How could this be his plan for the one he called "highly favored"? This doesn't look like favor at all.

The Bible tells us nothing of this inconvenient journey except that it happened. And it is in that void that I bite my lip, my brows furrowed. I glimpse and wonder, *God, why? Why must there be a difficult trek to Bethlehem—in Mary's life, and in mine? Why must the dust swirl and our feet swell? Why must the Messiah kick within us as we bump along? God, is there any purpose in the journey, any meaning in the daily trudge toward a place we cannot see and don't understand?*

I've been pregnant, but never on a donkey.

I've waddled down the driveway with sore legs and distended belly. But I've never walked nearly one hundred miles with a baby playing trampoline on my bladder.

I never would have dreamed of it. Maybe Mary didn't either.

But she went. She walked, she rode, she traveled on this path to the place God wanted her to be. She did it, and so must we. I wonder if it happened something like this:

Mary Tells Her Story

They say he's the son of god. They say it of Caesar Augustus, adopted son of Julius who they say is a god. Augustus. The Romans used to only use that name for their gods. But it's the emperor's name now. So they call him son of god, born in a palace in Rome, born to a king's brother, born of royalty, wearing a crown.

But my son, this one I carry in a womb now round and full, he is the *true* Son of God. He is the true Emperor, the true King.

And yet it is Caesar Augustus who exercises his authority from Rome and sets me on a path I never wished for. A journey to Bethlehem. It is a long journey, taking us nearly a week. We travel south. I walk, well, waddle really. And I ride like a sack of squash on the back of Joseph's old donkey. Months ago I practically ran to Elizabeth's. But now I go slowly — oh, so slowly — with my belly swaying before me, my feet fat and painful, and my back aching with every step.

Bethlehem.

Because Caesar Augustus has issued a decree and the whole Roman world must be counted.

The Roman world.

Don't they know it won't be Rome's anymore? It will belong to my God, to my son.

And yet I waddle, I ride, I bump and bumble along, and wonder, *Why now? Of all the times for Caesar to call for a census, why must it be when I am so pregnant that I can't even see my toes?*

The baby kicks. His tiny foot smashes into my ribs, and I gasp. He's a strong one, this boy. He turns and flips and rumbles, until my belly wobbles like a cup of wine in an old man's hand.

I glance at Joseph. He smiles at me, a sad but comforting tipping of his lips. He has done all he could to make this journey bearable. He is a good man. A righteous man. He would have divorced me quietly, but God sent him an angel in a dream. The angel said not to be afraid. So he wasn't.

I am trying not to be.

But I'm tired. My feet hurt. The journey is long. And now here we are, traveling this strange road to the City of David.

Why, Lord? Why now? Why couldn't I have stayed home where my mother could help me deliver my child? Where the midwife I've known all my life would have come to my side? Where everything is familiar, normal, easy? Why must I travel on this meaningless road, take this pointless journey, to a place I do not know and have never been?

Dust billows up before me, sticks in my eyelashes, wiggles down my throat. I want to go home.

But Joseph leads us on. Toward Jerusalem, and beyond it. Toward people I've never met, a place I've only heard about in stories. He leads me toward the unknown, and I stumble along, wishing, hoping that my God will still be there when I get to the end of the journey. When I get to Bethlehem.

The baby thrashes, and I press my hand against my belly. I suppose it is fitting that the Messiah will be born in David's town. The Messiah in Bethlehem. There is perhaps a prophecy … But oh, the journey is long. It's hard.

Lord, couldn't there have been an easier way?

A Painful Journey

How many times have I echoed Mary's possible questions in my own heart, my own life? *God, isn't there an easier way? Couldn't you have spared me from this meaningless, painful journey? Why must we go this way? Why can't I just stay home where it's comfortable and safe?*

This isn't the life I thought I signed up for!

Because sometimes the journey doesn't make any sense. Sometimes it hurts. Sometimes it seems to come at the worst possible moment. I know, because I've been on that road, the road to Bethlehem, where I'm following God's will, submitted to him, and still life is hard. The way is confusing and painful, and God doesn't intervene. He doesn't step in to make it easy.

> *The way is confusing and painful, and God doesn't intervene. He calls me to keep walking. He calls me to trust.*

He calls me to keep walking.

He calls me to trust.

When I committed my life to following Jesus, I never expected a difficult journey. I loved Jesus. Jesus loved me. He died for my sins, rose again, and had a wonder-filled plan for my life. All I needed to do was surrender and the adventure would begin, an adventure filled with a loving, Christ-following husband, three beautiful children, a ministry that would change the world, a boxer pup, and a white picket fence. Sure, there might be some obstacles to overcome, but in the end, it would all be songs and daisies and success.

Or not.

I wasn't prepared for "not." I got the loving, Christ-following husband, but my expectations of an easy journey turned to shattered shards when we tried for the three beautiful children.

Unlike Mary's, my unwanted journey was not an almost hundred-mile trek while pregnant. Instead, it was a years-long journey of *not* pregnant.

The Dreaded Word

After six years of marriage and having no children, I sat in my doctor's office and heard her mutter the dreaded word: *infertility*.

Really? Me? God's chosen? God's beloved? Infertile?

But that was his decree. A long journey through infertility. A journey I didn't want to take. Didn't want to accept.

But the King had spoken.

And so I listened as the doctor told me of tests and treatments, cycles and drugs and strange statistics. I listened and left with a hand full of pamphlets and a heart full of fear.

And I started down the difficult path of prodding tests, painful treatments, frequent failures, and far too many disappointments.

I watched and waited and wept as friends and family members became pregnant. I prayed and questioned as I read abortion statistics and wrestled with the justice of God. I learned to hate Mother's Day and to avoid people who would ask awkward questions. And I slogged on month after month, year after year, trying and failing and crying.

This wasn't the life of success and answered prayer I believed I would have. Didn't God love me? Didn't he have a wonderful plan for me? Didn't the coming of the Messiah in my life also mean all would be well?

No. Not for me.

For me it meant this journey through a pain that would, month-by-month, break my faith and leave it like bits of splintered glass scattered at my feet. It meant stumbling through a dozen doubts, a hundred fears, a thousand disappointments. It meant walking a path I didn't want and didn't understand. It meant wrestling with a God who could have ended my pain, my journey, at any moment ... but didn't.

And eventually it meant finding that same God in ways I never before imagined. It meant being crushed and remade. It meant discovering a wonder that I never would have believed possible.

Because, in the end, my journey through infertility was God's journey. It was his path, his plan, his purpose, his will that I travel the path to my own Bethlehem. And that I discover in the journey that I am changed by it. That Christ lives in me, and at the end of the road, I will see the face of my Savior.

As I sat in that doctor's office and tried to swallow that single word, *infertility*, was I prepared for the journey? No. Did I believe that God would use it for my good? No. Did I trust him and walk forward unafraid? No.

I trembled. I doubted. I feared. I questioned. I crumbled beneath the weight of the disappointments that I didn't know how to bear.

But I walked forward. I simply walked. And God walked with me. Every day. Every month. Every year.

For me, and for Mary, that was enough.

Mary's Journey

Too often, I think, when we approach the Christmas story, we are caught up in the star, the angels, the babe in the manger. We forget that it took a nearly one-hundred-mile journey, while pregnant, to get there.

If Mary and Joseph traveled through Samaria, it would have been eighty miles. But Jews traveling through Samaria weren't safe and were unlikely to get lodging, so Mary and Joseph may have taken the longer route in the Jordan Valley. They may have traveled with others or alone. They may have walked, or as tradition asserts, Joseph could have led his donkey while Mary rode. It could have taken four days if they went through Samaria and Joseph walked fast. It could have taken over a week if they went the long way and went slowly for Mary.

The Bible doesn't tell us. It doesn't say how they traveled or how long it took. It doesn't tell us if they had to stop every couple of hours for Mary to rest. It doesn't say how Mary felt or what Joseph did or that this was a hard, painful, difficult journey for a pregnant girl. It only tells us that they traveled to Bethlehem while Mary was pregnant. In stark, simple language, Luke 2:5 says, "He [Joseph] went there [to Bethlehem] to register with Mary, who was pledged to be married to him and was expecting a child." That's it. Mary went. By foot, by donkey, alone with Joseph, or in a caravan? We don't know. But we do know that they didn't travel by automobile on a paved road. We know it wasn't a two-hour jaunt on a pleasant day. It could not have been a simple journey.

And yet, despite the difficulty, nothing is mentioned about how God intervened to smooth their travels. There's nothing about being carried on angel's wings or being magically transported. Only that she went. The rest is up to us to discern, to consider, to ponder how God's declaration of Mary's blessedness started with a difficult journey, perhaps on donkey-back, while very pregnant.

Blessing does not mean "easy." It means challenge and pain and discomfort and sometimes danger.

Highly favored. Blessed. On the back of a donkey on a dusty journey away from home. I hold those two images in tension and realize that I must rethink the meaning of God's blessing in my life. Clearly, blessing does not mean "easy." It does not mean comfort and luxury and prosperity and ease. It means a difficult journey. It means challenge and pain and discomfort and sometimes danger.

That's the beginning of blessedness, of being highly favored by the Most High God.

An Emperor's Decree

I wonder what Mary thought as she dealt with all the aches and pains of pregnancy on the long road to Bethlehem. The last time we saw her in Luke's gospel account, she was singing of God's mercy and the downfall of the proud and powerful.

Wasn't Caesar supposed to be subject to her son? Wasn't proud Rome supposed to be taken down?

But, instead, we see the Roman emperor making a decree, requiring Mary bend to his will, sending her on a difficult trip. Here it looks like Caesar is in control. He is the one with the power. Where is God? Why doesn't he intervene?

He has. But it's possible that Mary couldn't see it. She couldn't see what we see in hindsight. How could she know that God himself had moved the emperor's hand? That God had long ago determined that the Messiah would be born in David's birthplace, in Bethlehem. Micah 5:2 says, "But you, Bethlehem Ephrathah, though you are small among the clans of Judah, out of you will come for me one who will be ruler over Israel, whose origins are from of old, from ancient times."

God had a plan. He knew what he was doing in the journey. "Rome was an unconscious agent in God's work. The profane decree of a census had yielded a divine event," says commentator Darrell Bock. If Herod had to go to his chief priests and teachers of the law to discover where the Messiah was to be born, it's likely that Mary wasn't thinking, *Of course, I know I have to go to Bethlehem so that the Messiah can be born there according to the prophet Micah.* And even if she was, wouldn't it have been easier for her to be living there already? For her family to have moved there when she was young? Or for her to simply have grown up there or moved anytime before being round with child?

But God didn't take the easy way. He didn't seem concerned with Mary's comfort at all. He could have intervened. But he didn't. So step after step, mile after mile, Mary traveled the difficult road not knowing, not understanding, but walking anyway. Walking with round belly, aching back, swollen feet.

And this time there would be no angel to explain or ease the way. No heavenly messenger to tell Mary of God's ultimate plan.

Mary simply had to go. One step at a time. Forward, to a place she did not know for a reason she most likely didn't understand.

She would just have to waddle forward, in faith, even when it didn't make sense.

But at the end of the journey, Mary would encounter Christ in a unique way. The Messiah would be born, and she would be transformed. She would hold God incarnate in her arms—but only after a long and arduous journey.

A Path We Don't Understand

It's no different for you or me. Sometimes we have to travel a path we don't understand to arrive in the place God wants us to be.

As I recall my journey and Mary's, they teach me that even through hurt and discomfort, maybe especially in hurt and pain, God is leading to a place where I will glimpse his glory anew. He is saying to me that I must travel the path he has placed before me in order to get to the place he has planned for me since the beginning.

So when you've surrendered to God's call and are suddenly thrust onto a road you never imagined and never wanted, remember, he knows the path you take. He travels with you, within you, and you will see him as you never could have before if you just keep going, trusting, and persevering.

There you will see the face of the Messiah. You will meet him in a new way. So place one foot in front of the other and walk through your life day by day, knowing that this road, as pointless as it seems, is the only way to his will.

Jesus must be born in Bethlehem. You must travel the difficult road at the worst time in your life to get there. Keep going, have faith, walk … and you will get to that new place where you will see him in a new way. The place where you will be changed. Don't give up. Don't despair.

This road leads to Bethlehem.

Who Is This God?

If God loves us, if he has called us, shouldn't he smooth our path? Shouldn't he make it easy to follow his will?

Apparently not, because our God is the God of the journey. He is not the God of the easy way. He has no easy button.

So why do we think things like, *If only I learned faster, What did I do to deserve this? Why is God punishing me?* or *I must be doing something wrong,* when the journey is long and difficult, when we don't arrive the moment we set out?

We forget that God knows what he's doing. He has planned our travels, foreseen our journey. And he has a purpose in it. He travels with us. Within us.

> *We forget that God knows what he's doing. He has foreseen our journey. And he has a purpose in it.*

The journey isn't punishment; it's God's narrow road for us. It's the way to his will. It's the difficult path to see him more clearly, to hold him in our arms, for him to be born in our lives in new and more vibrant ways.

Our God is the God of the journey. He is the God *in* the journey.

Consider the journeys of the major players in biblical history:

- Abraham traveled to the Promised Land.
- The Israelites traveled across the desert, and wandered in it, after their exodus from Egypt.
- Ruth traveled to Israel and became the great-grandmother of King David.
- Daniel traveled to Babylon.
- Mary traveled to Bethlehem.
- Jesus traveled from his throne in heaven to the dark, jostling womb of a woman.

God is the God *of* the journey and *in* the journey. He is the one who calls us to walk the narrow path, for his Son tells us, "Small is the gate and narrow the road that leads to life, and only a few find it" (Matt. 7:14). And of this road, he says, "Whether you turn to the right or to the left, your ears will hear a voice behind you, saying, 'This is the way; walk in it'" (Isa. 30:21).

So we walk, we stumble, we run — and we remember: the journey matters. God is in it. He has planned it from long ago that we might come to the place we need to be.

And he gives us encouragement.

From Paul: "I consider my life worth nothing to me; my only aim is to finish the race and complete the task the Lord Jesus has given me — the task of testifying to the good news of God's grace" (Acts 20:24). And: "Run in such a way as to get the prize" (1 Cor. 9:24).

And from the writer of Hebrews: "Let us run with perseverance the race marked out for us, fixing our eyes on Jesus, the pioneer and perfecter of faith" (12:1–2).

I read these verses, and I take a breath. I hold it then let it go. I can run this race, I can finish this journey. I can walk this path God has set before me and someday arrive in Bethlehem.

I can do it because I am Mary. You are Mary. We travel a road we don't understand to a place we don't know. We walk, we waddle, we bumble along. And Jesus walks with us. He is in us.

The journey isn't easy, but we are not alone.

God is whispering in our ear: *If there was another way to get you to where you need to be, I would have taken it. This is the only path. This dusty, rocky road is my will for you. Walk in it. Trust me, and travel to your Bethlehem. I am the God of the journey. I am the God in the journey. Walk with me.*

CHAPTER 4

Life in the Barn
The Birth of a Savior

LUKE 2:6 – 7

Today I'm setting out my little Precious Moments nativity set on my mantel. I put out the tiny manger, set around the cow, the donkey, the palm tree. I place the shepherd with his sheep to the left and the wise men with their gifts to the right. Carefully, oh so carefully, I set baby Jesus in the center. He's sleeping, his cheeks pink, his blankets a gentle polka-dotted pastel. I put Joseph beside him, and then I pick up the kneeling Mary.

I hold her in my hand. She is sweet and perfect, her eyes dark, her head bowed. Pristine. Her gown is spotless, a pale buttercup yellow. Her head covering falls in perfect folds, with not a smudge to mar her serene expression.

Just as if she hadn't just completed a hundred-mile journey while pregnant. As if she hadn't been turned away from an actual room. As if she hadn't spent hours in painful labor. As if there was no blood, no dirt, no sweat, no stink. As if she never really gave birth in a barn.

I set her there beside the sleeping Jesus, knowing that we have it all wrong. It isn't in the sweet pastels of life that we find Jesus, that we encounter him in a new way. He isn't born in our sterile birthing rooms. He isn't wrapped in soft, sweet-smelling fleece. He isn't in the carefully structured, pleasantly perfect places we like to create for him.

Instead, we find him in the stink, in the noise, in the out-of-the-way, hard, sticky, smelly places of life.

No, Jesus is not born in our palaces, or even in our guest rooms. He's born in our life-barns. He's born in the place where nothing seems right, where nothing is as we think it should be.

That's the real Jesus — born in a barn, wrapped in rags, laid in a feeding trough.

I imagine it happened something like this:

Mary Tells Her Story

There's no place for us. No place for this babe, this Son of the almighty God, that I bear.

But the pains come anyway. Sharp, insistent. *Not now*, I want to say. *Not yet. There is no place for you. Nowhere for you to be born.*

But my womb clenches again, and I gasp. The pains are more regular now, radiating into my back. He will not wait, this divine baby of mine.

Joseph approaches me, places a hand on my tight belly. He shakes his head.

No place for us.

I nearly double over. I pant. Quickly, heavily.

"There is a place with the animals," he whispers.

I swallow. Hard. Is it possible that this child, the Messiah, the King of all kings, will be born in a barn? *No . . .*

Lord, is there nowhere else? Can you find no other place for your own Son?

But the heavens are silent. No guest room, no spare closet, no private corner in a relative's home.

And the pain comes again.

Joseph takes my arm. "We must hurry."

"Not the stable."

"It's the only place. I'm sorry."

I'm sorry too. *Oh, Lord . . .*

Step by step, stopping to breathe, to not breathe, to groan, I make my way toward the animals.

And then we are there. In the rustling, the stink, the dirt, the mud. No midwife. No friend. No mother. Just me. Just Joseph. And *them*.

A donkey brays.

A cow lifts its tail.

A horse stomps and spreads four legs.

No, not here . . .

I lie on the filthy straw. I pant. I cry.

A horse nickers, pushes at an empty feeding trough.

I swat a fly. And the pain comes again.

This time I scream. I wheeze. I gasp. And my mind floods with ripping agony. Ten seconds. Twenty. Thirty. A minute. And more.

Joseph grabs the rags. I am sweating now. He wipes my brow. But there is nothing he can do. He cannot share this pain.

No one can.

My belly contracts. Hard. I clench my teeth. Bite back my shouts.

It hurts. Oh, Lord, it hurts so much.

My sweat, mixed with the smell of horse urine and cow dung. The snuffling of a donkey. The frightened glance of a husband who is not the baby's father.

Help, Lord!

A rush of water runs down my legs. Minutes turn to hours. Hours of shocking pain and moments of panting relief. On and on.

The pain. Mind-numbing. Middle-ripping. Pain.

And the pressure.

Finally, the baby is coming. I scream at Joseph. But he is ready.

I am half-squatting, half-lying.

"Push," he yells.

I push.

I yell.

I breathe. Breathe in the rank stink. Breathe in the smell of blood. Breathe in the scent of things that no king should smell.

But this King will.

Oh, God, will he really be born in a barn? Your Son? The hope of all Israel?

I push. And rest. And push. And yell. And push. And cry. And push. And groan.

It is no easy thing to birth a Savior.

"I see his head!" Joseph's eyes are wide. His hands ready.

I bear down. Hard.

And the baby comes. A King, sliding into this world covered in vernix and blood, and surrounded by animals as the only witnesses to this moment that will change the world.

Joseph laughs.

The baby wails.

And I weep.

I weep for a promise born in a barn. I weep for a Messiah born in the stink. I weep for a King crowned not with gold but with blood. Will it always be so?

Joseph cuts the baby's cord. He presses my stomach, and the afterbirth spews from me.

It is done, this birthing of a Savior.

Joseph wipes him with a rag and hands him to me. I gather him in my arms. He looks so normal, this Son of God. So ordinary. So small, this tiny babe, with a shock of dark hair, a red face, and wrinkled, old-man skin. This is the one we've waited for.

I close my eyes and kiss his forehead.

He squirms and squawks at me.

I wrap this ordinary, extraordinary baby in rags and place him in the empty feeding trough. A box made for the animals to eat becomes his bed. He looks around, dark gray eyes taking in a world gone awry.

What must it be like for God to see through the eyes of a human babe? To smell through a human nose? To feel the scratch of the rags, the hardness of the board?

But he doesn't cry. Not at this moment.

He just looks.

He sees.

And my eyes blur.

There is the King of all kings, the Son of God himself, wrapped in rags and lying in a feeding trough. A Messiah surrounded by stink. But somehow I don't smell it anymore.

I laugh. I laugh at the incongruity. I laugh at the wildness of my God.

I laugh, because the God of the universe took this barn and turned it into a palace. He took what should not be and filled it with wonder.

Wonder in the Barn

And that's the beauty of a babe born in a barn. From the moment Jesus arrived, he transformed. He transformed a stable into a birthplace for a King, an old feeding trough into a royal bassinet, and a poor young woman into the mother of the Messiah.

From the moment Jesus arrived, he transformed.

I think that's how it always is. Jesus is not born in our pastel palaces. He doesn't enter our lives looking for the places that are pretty or easy or comfortable. Instead, he is born in our life-barns — in the stink, in the noise, in the places where nothing is as it should be. That's where God comes to us in a new, more vibrant way, and changes us. Those are the places where wonder is born, where beauty is discovered, where the God of all the universe breaks through to hold us in his arms.

Jerome, a fourth-century theologian, wrote in his *On the Nativity of the Lord*, "He found no room in the Holy of Holies that shone with gold, precious stones, pure silk and silver. He is not born in the midst of gold and riches but in the midst of dung, in a stable where our sins were filthier than the dung. He is born on a dunghill in order to lift up those who come from it: 'From the dunghill he lifts up the poor.'"

I encountered this strange dichotomy one ordinary Sunday morning at church. That day I learned that only God can transform the awkward, noisy, seemingly out-of-place things in life into something beautiful, something filled with incredible wonder.

Andy showed me that. He inspired my novel *Shades of Morning*; he taught me how to see; he changed me into more of who God created me to be. Andy showed me beauty in the barn — in the awkward, noisy place where things aren't quite right.

The Wonder of Andy

It was a regular Sunday morning at church. People wandered down the aisles, sat in their padded chairs, smiled at newcomers, read their bulletins. Gentle music played in the perfectly lit sanctuary. So like a room where you'd expect Christ to be born.

But that was soon to change. Andy would change it.

I walked into church and sat down in my usual seat, halfway back from the front and on the right side of the church platform. Soon the singing began. Then some announcements. Then another song. Comfortable, just like always. Then we came to the third song in the worship set. Something about our God of wonders. I sang quietly, as I do every Sunday, because my husband tells me I can't carry a tune. I didn't want to disturb the other worshipers. Everything was going so smoothly. So ... carpet and cushy chairs. So unlike a stinky, noisy barn. Everything was going as it was supposed to go.

The second verse flipped onto the screen in front. Everyone sang just like they were supposed to. Everyone clapped at the right moment, in time with the music. And a few people even swayed a bit in their seats.

Until Andy.

At the third verse, a noise came from the far side of the church. A loud noise. More like a squawk, a sound you might hear from an animal. Strange and unexpected—the barn broke into the comfort of the carpeted room. And then the sound grew louder. I furrowed my brow. Was that someone singing ... badly?

I stood on tiptoes and peeked toward the sound.

And there was Andy. His arms were raised. His eyes were closed. And he was singing to his God for all he was worth. Andy, in his middle teens, with blond hair, thick glasses, and small ears. Andy, with Down syndrome and a grin on his face big enough for the angels to see. Andy, shout-singing with all his might through that radiant smile.

I watched and listened, and I had to smile too. A small smile at first. Then, like Andy's singing, my smile grew. And grew. And grew. Because at that moment, I knew I was seeing something precious, beautiful, special. I was getting a glimpse of something far beyond the ordinary. Something fit for heaven itself. I was seeing the face of God.

For a brief instant, the music faltered, the other voices hushed just a bit. And then the guitar strummed again, the congregation's voices surged, and I knew that some, at least, had seen what I had. They'd witnessed the wonder, beheld the beauty, of a soul in love with his God. They'd seen Jesus in a new way.

Andy transformed our comfortable sanctuary into a barn, and we found the Messiah born there. We saw his face in the glow of Andy's. We encountered the Christ.

That moment changed me. It showed me that beauty is found in unexpected places, and that God's gifts in our lives are often wrapped in awkward, off-key packages. I witnessed something beautiful, something wondrous that day, and it made me see that so often the hard things in life, the things we want to hide away, to forget, to cover up, can be transformed into things of beauty in the hands of God.

And that's the kind of upside-down, inside-out wonder I find in the Christmas story, the story of a God born in a stinky stable, wrapped in rags, laid in a crusty feeding trough. How could it be?

Born in a Stable?

There's so much about the story that we don't know. Luke's description is stark in its simplicity. "The account of Jesus' birth is spare in the extreme," says John Nolland. And commentator Fred Craddock adds, "How simple and bare it all seems."

All we know is this: "It came about, while they were there, the days were fulfilled for her to bear. And she bore her firstborn son and she *esparganosen* the babe, and put him in a *phatne* because there was not a place for them in the *katalumati*" (Luke 2:6–7, translation mine).

First, Mary *esparganosen*, which means she took strips of rags and wrapped them around Jesus' tiny body as was the custom for keeping the limbs straight. She cared for him. She did what she could for him to have a healthy start in life. Would a mother like this want to bear her son in a stable? Not hardly. And yet that is what God chose.

She laid him in a *phatne*, a feeding trough for animals. Not a beautiful crèche filled with sweet-smelling straw but a wooden feeding trough filled with dried-up animal slobber, bits of stuck-on feed, and probably gnaw marks where a restless equine had taken a chunk or two out of the panels. I have nearly a dozen feeding troughs, and I can say for certain that they are not clean, sweet-smelling, or anything like the comfy cloth bassinets I used for my children. I would never lay my baby in a trough. But Mary had to. God had provided no other place. For Mary, for Joseph, for the shepherds who would soon come, the Son of God, the long-awaited Messiah, would be found in a dirty, smelly feeding trough. That's the kind of God we have.

Because there was not a place for them in the *katalumati*. This word doesn't mean Motel 6. It's not a formal inn made for travelers. When Luke wanted to indicate a formal inn (as in the parable of the good Samaritan in Luke 10:34), he used the word *pandocheion*, an entirely different term. *Katalumati*, however, is used by Luke to describe the upper guest room that Jesus used for his last Passover meal (the Last Supper) before he was arrested, beaten, and crucified.

Many were traveling to Bethlehem for the census. Relatives were opening their homes and offering their guest rooms to extended family. Rooms were filling. Cousins and uncles and distant relatives were coming together in homes — until there was no more room. No room for a carpenter from Nazareth, his very pregnant wife, and the babe she would soon bear. Even though that babe was God's own Son. No one could help. Relatives sometimes let us down. So do friends. So do strangers. People don't always step forward to make life easy. But neither Mary nor Luke placed any blame or expectation on the residents of Bethlehem. And neither should we when others don't step forward to make room for us. Because, just as in Mary's case, perhaps it was God's will that his Son be born in a barn. Perhaps it is God's will that you find him anew in the strange, stinky, this-isn't-right places of life.

Perhaps it is God's will that you find him anew in the strange, stinky, this-isn't-right places of life.

In scholarly circles, there's much debate on what kind of animal lodging Mary went to in order to birth Jesus. We know she was with the animals because she laid him in a feeding trough. But where was the trough? Was it an animal area in the lower portion of a home with an already crowded guest room? Was it out in the public square of town? Was it an overhang attached to a house where animals found shelter? Was it a cave, as set forth in a tradition that can be traced back to the midsecond century? Early Christian apologist Justin Martyr, in his *Dialogue with Trypho*, mentions the cave, as does the *Protoevangelium of James*, also from the second century. Origen, in the third century, wrote that the cave's location was known and therefore could very well be the same place where the Church of the Nativity stands today.

Wherever Jesus was laid, we know there was a feeding trough, and where there's a feeding trough, there are animals. And where there are animals, there are poop and pee and flies and dirt and noise and just plain yuck.

Having a baby in a barn was never part of Mary's birthing plan. Using a feeding trough for a crib wasn't in the plan either. Born in a barn, wrapped in rags, laid in a feeding trough ...

That was not how it was supposed to be. How could that possibly be Mary's vision of the birth of the King of Kings?

It wasn't.

"If we imagine that Jesus was born in a freshly swept, county fair stable, we miss the whole point. It was wretched—scandalous! There was sweat and pain and blood and cries as Mary reached up to the heavens for help," says Kent Hughes.

This birth wasn't anything like Mary would have wanted or expected. It was a problem. It was all wrong. And yet that is where she found the Son of God. That is when she first heard his cries, first held him in her arms, first encountered him in a more vivid, more wondrous way. It was here that she became the mother of the Messiah.

It is the same for you and for me. Just like Mary, we take our first steps in becoming who we were meant to be in the far-from-perfect portions of life. In the difficulties, in the stink, in the places that are not where we want to be. Where we least expect it, where we least want to be, there the Messiah meets us. There he is revealed in new ways. In life's stables—in the defeats, rejections, disappointments, screams of pain, frustrations of labor, and sweat of trying and failing—Jesus is there. God is coming in a new way to transform the barn into a birthplace of the King.

So, embrace the barn ... and find the Christ born anew in the very place where life stinks.

Who Is This God?

Who is this God whose Son was born in a stable? Who is he who was found by lowly shepherds lying in an animal's feeding trough, dressed not in robes but in rags? Who is he who comes to the place we don't expect and looks so unlike what we imagined?

He is the God of the barn.

We encounter him in places we don't expect him to be. Consider the following biblical encounters:

- Job encountered God in a storm while sitting on an ash heap (Job 2:8; 38:1).

- Abraham encountered God outside the wicked city of Sodom in the heat of the day (Gen. 18:1).
- Jacob encountered God alone in the darkness, in the middle of the night (Gen. 32:22–24).
- Moses encountered God in the wilderness, on the far side of the desert (Ex. 3:1).
- Elijah encountered God in the cave while running for his life (1 Kings 19:9).
- Shadrach, Meshach, and Abednego encountered God in the fire (Dan. 3:25).
- And Mary encountered him in a stable …

God's glory is revealed in unexpected places. It is seen in the storm, from the ash heap, at the edge of a wicked city, in the heat, in the darkness, in the wilderness, in the cave, in the fires of life. There we find him. In the barn.

The angel's words to the shepherds echo down through the centuries to us. God whispers, "You will find a baby wrapped in cloths and lying in a manger" (Luke 2:12). Because Jesus is born where life stinks. He comes to us not in our palaces but in the stinky, smelly, dirty, unadorned places in life. And there, only there, do we discover something deep and wondrous about the God we follow. We discover that he is the God who takes our life-yuck and transforms it. He takes the places in life where nothing is as we wanted it to be and makes them the very place we encounter the Messiah born in us.

In life's stink, mess, noise, dirt, and poking straw …

- He is the God of stink.
- He is the God of mess.
- He is the God of noise.
- He is the God of dirt.
- He is the God of discomfort.
- He is the God of the barn.

This is the real God—born in the stink, in the noise, in the places that are not as they should be. Born to transform them in you, in me.

So, come, the angels are singing. God is calling. *You will find me in the stable...*

CHAPTER 5

Embracing Mystery
Pondering the Shepherds' Visit

LUKE 2:16 – 19

I *don't know.*
　　Scary words. I don't like to speak them. I don't like to write them. I don't like them at all. Instead, I much prefer:
I know.
I understand.
It makes sense.
I have the answers.
But the reality of life often is:
I don't know.
I don't understand.
It doesn't make sense.
I don't have the answers.
　　I cringe away from admissions like that. I want my world to make sense. I want explanations and reasons and a carefully constructed theology where all the *i*'s are diligently dotted and all the *t*'s carefully crossed.
　　I don't want mystery.

And yet God is a God of mystery. He often refuses to explain himself and instead woos me to that uncomfortable in-between place where things don't make sense and I don't have it all figured out.

> *God is a God of mystery. He often woos me to that uncomfortable in-between place where things don't make sense.*

He beckons me there and asks me not to understand but instead to ponder.

To question.

To think.

To wonder.

I suppose I shouldn't be surprised. After all, this is the God who calls me to live in the tension between faith and works, between a loving God and a broken world, between justice and mercy. He calls me to wrestle with my questions, dance with my doubts, and live with not understanding all the whys and wherefores and what-does-it-all-means.

He calls me to ponder as he offers no easy answers, no pat theologies, no simple explanations to put on the bumper stickers of my life.

He beckons me to live with mystery—the mystery of a Messiah in a manger.

Mystery.

Mary pondered the mystery of her God when scruffy shepherds showed up looking for an infant lying where the animals feed. She pondered as they told a strange story of singing angels who visited not a newborn Messiah but a bunch of sheepherders in the fields. She pondered as they spoke. And she treasured the truths she could not yet understand.

Perhaps it happened something like this ...

Mary Tells Her Story

I hold him in my arms. He nestles and nuzzles. So normal. So real. He lets out a cry, his mouth open, searching.

I smile and guide him to eat. He is strong, this newborn son of mine. Of God's. This Messiah.

I roll the word over in my mind as I gaze down at his pink cheeks, his shock of curly black hair. His eyes are closed, his lashes dark against his skin.

Messiah. Rescuer. Deliverer. Redeemer. King ... *Baby.*

I sigh and place him back in the manger. He wiggles. Hay rustles. I press it down to make it softer around him.

A Messiah in a manger. What does it mean?

I lean over and kiss his brow. "Will the wild ox consent to serve you? Will it stay by your manger at night?" I whisper the words from the holy scroll of Job, words spoken by God himself.

Does God see his Son in a manger? Did he intend to provide no better bed? Will there be no visit from angels bearing gifts? Will there be no witnesses to the miracle of his birth?

Lord, where are the angels?

I hear a noise behind me. A rustling of feet. A whisper of voices.

"Here."

"We found him."

"Just as they said."

I turn and see the silhouettes of men against the night sky. Men in ragged robes with tall staffs in their hands.

These are no angels. They are shepherds.

Simple shepherds from the fields. Are these the witnesses God would send?

Joseph stands, positions himself between the shepherds and the babe. He touches my shoulder.

One man steps closer. "May we enter? May we see the baby?"

Joseph nods. I scoot closer to the manger.

The shepherds shuffle in. The smells of grass and dirt, sweat and sheep swirl in with them. I look into dirty faces, gaze at calloused hands gripping rough wood. I see the stains on their robes, the dirt caked on their sandals.

They are anything but angels.

And they bear no gifts.

Or do they?

Three lean over the feeding trough and laugh. They laugh!

"It's just as the angel told us," says the tallest.

"A baby in a manger."

"A Messiah in a feeding trough." The oldest sighs, his face alight with the incongruity of a Messiah-babe lying in a feeding trough for oxen.

I touch his sleeve. "An angel, you say? An angel visited you?"

"We were out in the fields, watching our flocks by night. An angel of the Lord appeared right before us. The glory of the Lord shone all around us. It was amazing."

"You mean it was terrifying." The tall shepherd moves closer and continues the story. "But he told us to not be afraid because he was bringing us good news. Us, shepherds living in the fields!"

The third shepherd shifts, never taking his eyes from my son. "He said the Messiah had been born, and the sign to us was to be the craziest thing I've ever heard — a baby wrapped in rags and lying in a feeding trough. He said we'd find the Messiah in a manger." He glances up. "And we did."

"Other angels came, a whole host of them. They sang of glory and peace. They sang of wonder."

"And when they left us, we came here, searching for a baby in the last place we'd have thought to find him."

"So here we are."

"And here he is." The last shepherd's voice drops low with awe.

Here he is ...

I sit back on my heels and wrestle with my own incongruities.

Welcomed by shepherds, not kings or angels ...

Angels singing not to him but to the low ones of our society in the open fields at night ...

Lying not in a crib but a manger ...

And that, somehow, is a sign.

Of what?

What kind of Messiah is this? What kind of Rescuer? What kind of King?

I stare at the old wooden feeding trough and grapple with the truth of God sending shepherds to a manger.

We put him there because we had no other place. God put him there because he intended to. Because it is a sign.

Not an accident. Not an oversight. But a sign.

A sign I cannot yet understand.

A Messiah meant to lie in a manger. Could it be? The words of the prophet Isaiah tiptoe through my mind: "The ox knows its master, the donkey its owner's manger, but Israel does not know, my people do not understand."

I don't know. I do not understand. But I do know there's meaning in the manger. God has done this. He has placed his Son in a feeding trough on purpose.

Will I ever comprehend it?

The shepherds rise, murmuring about all the people they must tell of this miracle. I watch them go, their robes swaying at their feet, their staffs tapping the ground with eager anticipation. And I know they'll speak of angels and a baby. Of feeding troughs and swaddling rags.

They'll speak of God.

But what kind of God is this? What kind of Messiah?

Their voices fade. I pick up my son again. I look into his slumbering face. There's so much I don't understand. So much that doesn't make sense at all. Will I ever make sense of a King born in a barn? Of a Messiah welcomed by shepherds? Of a Son of God with a manger for his bed?

I press my lips together and look out into the night. What do I do with these strange truths? How do I comprehend them?

I close my eyes and hold him close. I know what I will do. I will wrap these thoughts, these wonderings, carefully in the rags of my pondering and tuck them safely in the manger in my heart. There I will treasure them.

Because the shepherds brought a gift, after all. They brought the gift of Mystery.

The Wonder of Mystery

God doesn't promise us understanding. He doesn't promise that everything will make sense to us. Instead, he asks us to embrace the mysteries of our lives in him. He asks us to trust even when we don't understand. He asks us to wonder and wrestle, to ponder and grapple with the meaning of things that seem strange, out of place, and sometimes even inconsistent with our ideas of a loving God.

God doesn't promise us understanding. He asks us to trust even when we don't understand.

I know, because he asks me to do that very thing every time I think of my father.

A Little Girl's Daddy

I have very few memories of my biological dad. Just a few snap-shots in my mind of a man who held my hands, loved baseball, and brought me squeaky toys on his way home from work. But one memory I have is quite clear.

My dad sat in his favorite black vinyl recliner with his feet up and the sun streaming through the window behind him. On the opposite wall, the Dodgers played on our old rabbit-eared TV. My dad loved those Dodgers. Even at two years old, I knew it. And I knew my dad loved me too. What I didn't know was how much it would take for him to get mad at me. But I aimed to find out.

I marched over to the TV, looked at it, then looked at my dad, and stepped in front of the screen. I spread out my legs. I spread out my arms. And I waited.

"Marlo, please move." His voice was calm, gentle.

I didn't move.

"Marlo. Please move away. I want to see the game."

I stood my ground.

Twice more he asked me.

Twice more I stood, unmoving.

Then he tipped forward in his chair. The recliner's footrest snapped down.

And that's all I saw.

I ran as fast as I could go away from the TV, down the hall, into my room, and onto my little bed.

My dad didn't follow. He didn't need to. I was happy. I knew I was loved. And I knew there were limits. All was right in my world.

But it didn't last.

Because that is the final memory I have of my dad. I don't remember being told months later that he'd died of a heart attack while playing basketball. I don't remember a funeral. I don't remember a casket.

But today when I look back at pictures, I see a wide-eyed two-and-a-half-year-old with curly brown hair and no hint of a smile. I see a little girl who looks sad. Confused. Lost. I see someone who doesn't understand what's happened. Whose little life doesn't make sense anymore.

I cry as I hold her pictures in my hand and look into those round, dry eyes. Because I know that little girl. She still lives in me. And sometimes she still doesn't understand. Sometimes she's still a little lost, a little confused, a little sad.

And God, through Mary's journey, tells me that that's okay. Because he knows that little girl too. And he loves her.

Living with Mystery

Life doesn't have to make sense. We don't always have to understand. I still don't understand why I had to lose my father at two years old. It still doesn't make sense to me that that's the path God would choose for my life.

But I know God did choose it. It happened on purpose. Not because God was sleeping or he'd turned away. And not because he didn't care enough to save my father. God knew ... and a little girl lost her daddy.

And that is a mystery I must live with, a mystery I must grapple with — and somehow embrace. I can't just put it out of my mind or make up explanations to cling to or make excuses for God. Instead, I have to hold the truths of God's love and a father's death in my hands and treasure them both. I need to be able to say, "I don't know. I don't understand," as I think deeply and live with the tension of truths that seem at odds with each other, at odds with the way I want life to be, the way I want God to be. Someday I may understand. Someday I may not.

But either way, I must receive the gift of mystery and hold it close in my heart.

Mary's Mysteries

Mary had her mysteries too. We see it most clearly in the visit of the shepherds.

The encounter with the shepherds is told in simple terms. They hurried to Bethlehem to find Mary, Joseph, and the baby, who was lying in the manger. And when they had seen him, they went off and told everyone what they had seen and heard. People were amazed.

But they weren't transformed. They were simply wowed by a wow-worthy story.

Mary, however, didn't say, "Wow." Instead, she said, "Hmm ..."
Why?

Because I think she saw the incongruities.

She didn't just take a glance at a babe in a manger. She held him, encountered him, and so was able to see the truth—that the angel's proclamation, "A Savior has been born to you; he is the Messiah" (v. 11) did not sit comfortably with "You will find a baby wrapped in cloths and lying in a manger" (v. 12). A Messiah should not be in a manger. That just doesn't make sense.

So Mary treasured up what she had heard and seen, and she pondered it in her heart. In the Greek, the word for "ponder" also means "to bring together, to meet." So we have the idea of Mary bringing together disparate ideas in her mind and mulling over what they might mean.

She grappled with ideas that didn't easily come together and make sense, because she encountered, as a babe in a manger, a God who does not always make sense. She encountered a God who asked her not to have everything figured out with tidy explanations and clear conclusions but to wrestle with the mysteries of who this Messiah-God really was.

Here are just a few mysteries to be treasured, to be pondered:

• Angels who don't come to sing for their King but show up to shepherds. Now that doesn't make sense. David Garland says, "Surprisingly, that glory [of the angels' appearance] does not appear in the temple in nearby Jerusalem. Nor does it shine around the manger and the newborn child. Instead, it appears in an open field to lowly shepherds faithfully keeping watch over their sheep."

- A Messiah lying in a feeding trough. Now that doesn't make sense. St. Francis of Assisi wrote in a letter: "Though he was wealthy beyond reckoning, he still willingly chose to be poor with his blessed mother." And we know that God intended it that way because the angel sent the shepherds not to a barn or a house or a street or an address but to a manger. "This will be a sign to you," he said. "You will find a baby wrapped in cloths and lying in a manger" (v. 12).
- A Redeemer in rags. Now that doesn't make sense. Seventh-century English monk Bede wrote, "It should be noted that the sign given of the Savior's birth is not a child enfolded in Tyrian purple, but one wrapped with rough pieces of cloth."

If, like Mary, we are close enough to Jesus to hold him, to be near him, to be in a real relationship with him, we, too, will encounter mystery. We come up against truths that are hard to reconcile but are true all the same. We have to wrestle and wonder. Treasure and ponder.

> *If, like Mary, we are close enough to Jesus to hold him, to be near him, we, too, will encounter mystery.*

But if, like the shepherds, we travel only once to the manger, take a glance to corroborate what we've been told, then leave to do other tasks (even good ones), then we will see the baby and confirm what we'd hoped to be true. But we will miss the mystery. We will not encounter the deeper things of God. We will have no treasure to ponder.

Having No Answers

So often we think that the closer we are to Christ, the more answers we must have. But Mary teaches us that is not necessarily true. The shepherds had no questions, no doubts, no wonderings. But Mary did. The one who carried him in her womb and held him in her arms was the one who had no answers. She was the one who pondered the paradoxes and treasured them in her heart.

She was called to live with the mystery of a Messiah who was already so different from what she could have imagined. She pondered and treasured the mystery of things that could not yet make sense.

The question is, will we? Garland points out, "The Holy Spirit does not overshadow Mary to give her divine insight to understand what everything means. It is sometimes hard to see what God is doing when one is living in the midst of the events."

So why is it that so often we feel we need to make explanations for what God is doing in our lives and in the lives of those around us? If the shepherds came to us, would we explain why the babe was in a feeding trough? Would we excuse the stink, the poverty, the rough rags, and splintered wood? Would we spout platitudes or deny the strangeness of what is true?

Would we say:

"It's not really that bad." *(It's not really a feeding trough.)*

"I don't mind." *(I didn't want a real room.)*

"God is good, so I have nothing to complain about." *(These aren't really rags.)*

What if instead we saw God for who he really is? The God who provides only a trough for his own Son's crib. The God who sends shepherds to a baby wrapped in rags. The God who leaves heaven to become a baby in poverty. The God who does things in our lives that we don't understand, that don't seem to make sense, that aren't supposed to ... yet.

Who Is This God?

Who is this God who wraps himself in rags, who wraps himself in mystery? Who is this God who sends shepherds with a profound gift, the gift of wondering?

This is not the God of explanations and excuses.

This is the God of the manger.

He is the God who sent Abraham to Mount Moriah to make a sacrifice of his son, Isaac, the miraculous promised child of his elderly wife, Sarah. Abraham climbed the mountain and did not understand. He prepared the altar, laid Isaac on the altar, and raised the knife. And he did not understand. God provided a ram caught in a thicket to sacrifice in place of Isaac. Did Abraham ever understand the test? Did he comprehend that when he said, "God himself will provide the lamb" (Gen. 22:8), he was foreshadowing Christ on the cross, our baby in the manger? Could he see that the ram in the thicket was a symbol of a sacrificed Messiah? I don't think so. But Abraham embraced the mystery and obeyed, even though his God did not come with lengthy explanations or soft reassurances.

He is the God who told his prophet Isaiah, "Go and tell this people: 'Be ever hearing, but never understanding; be ever seeing, but never perceiving'" (Isa. 6:9). God called him to preach to a people who would not hear, would not change. Why? Did Isaiah understand that in all his failures to get through to his people, he would paint a picture of the coming Messiah? Did he understand that when he spoke words that would not change the hardened hearts of a stubborn people, he was showing you and me, thousands of years later, who the Messiah was meant to be? I don't think so. But he preached, he prophesied, he obeyed anyway. He embraced the mystery of his God.

He is the God who wrapped a towel around his waist, knelt before Simon Peter, and embodied the incongruity of God-Messiah-King as a lowly servant who washes feet. And he said to

Peter, "You do not realize now what I am doing, but later you will understand" (John 13:7). He says the same to us. He says it with a towel around his waist and a basin in his hand. He says, "You don't have to understand now. You don't have to have the answers. Just trust me."

Our God is the God who asks us to ponder, to wait, to trust when we don't understand, when life doesn't make sense.

Our God is the God who asks us to ponder, to wait, to trust when we don't understand, when life doesn't make sense.

When shepherds appear in the doorway ...

When angels don't come to you ...

When you have to lay your baby in a feeding trough because God didn't provide a crib ...

When all you have is rags ...

When a toddler's dad dies ...

When you don't have it all figured out ...

God calls us not to make up explanations but to ponder, simply to ponder. And treasure the truths in our hearts. He calls us to wonder.

So ...

What if we pondered instead of excused?

What if we treasured instead of denied?

What if we wrestled instead of explained?

What if we embraced the mystery of our God?

What if we did so not only in our own mysteries but also when we walked with others through theirs?

Then we would see the real Christ. We would encounter the babe in the manger. And we could hear the angels sing. Because good news often looks so different from what we would have imagined. Good news is often found in a feeding trough.

Can you find him there? Can you find the joy hidden in the manger?

Bethlehem has opened Eden: Come, let us see!

We have found joy hidden! Come, let us take possession of the paradise within the cave....

Let us hasten to this place where for our sake the eternal God was born as a little child!

From the Ikos of the Nativity of the Lord

And that, in itself, is the most profound mystery of all. Will you find the joy of that mystery; will you draw near in the paradox? Will you embrace this kind of God? Will you ...

wrestle,
wait,
and wonder?

CHAPTER 6

The Soul-Piercing Sword

Simeon's Blessing

LUKE 2:22 – 35

An angel called her favored. A cousin called her blessed, the most blessed of all women. And now another would speak the Spirit's words to Mary as she came to the temple with a babe, a Savior, in her arms.

It is here she would encounter ...

> the Spirit's promise,
> an old man's hope,
> and a blessing unlike any that had come before,
> the blessing of a soul-piercing sword.

It is interludes like this that stop me, shock me, and send strange shivers into my soul. It is in these moments when the Spirit speaks words of beauty, of grace ... of suffering, that I see and know that I am wrong about God when I envision him. My God is too pleasant, too comfortable.

My God is too nice.

Mary's God was not. I need to see as she saw. I need to hear Simeon's song and have my heart quiver, my hair stand on end.

This God—conceived in a virgin, born incarnate in a barn, named on the eighth day, held in an old man's arms—he is not a tame God. He is not a jolly old man in the sky.

He is the God of wonder. He is the God of suffering. And he calls me to walk at his side.

So I approach this strange interlude with trembling. And Simeon's words of blessing—*blessing?*—echo in my spirit: "A sword will pierce your own soul" (v. 35). A sword, a sign of warfare, judgment, but mostly of pain, of death. Does God really expect Mary to hear the portent of suffering as a blessing? Does he expect that from me?

I wonder these things as I read the story of a faithful girl doing what was right and following God's will with all her heart. I read. I ponder. And wonder ...

Am I supposed to suffer too?

It may have happened much like this:

> *This God— conceived in a virgin, born in a barn, named on the eighth day, held in an old man's arms—he is not a tame God.*

Mary Tells Her Story

Everything must be right for the presentation of this child, this Son of God, this Messiah of my people, Israel. It will be according to the law of my fathers. "Every male who first opens the womb shall be called holy to the Lord," the Law says. Especially this one.

So we have come to the great city of Jerusalem, the city where David reigned, where Solomon was visited by the kings and queens of the world. The city of promise. Of royalty. Of hope.

The streets bustle with merchants and men hurrying to market. Children play. Women walk, discreet with heads covered. The sound is like water rushing as I hear the cries of beggars and see the booths where some of my own people collect taxes for Rome. Things will be different now. The Messiah has come. He has come as a babe to his city for the very first time.

The significance shivers through my soul.

And then the temple looms before us. Grand and beautiful, stones massive in size. But it is still not what it once was. And I think, *Someday, someday ... because my son has come ...*

But first we will offer a sacrifice according to the Law. We will do what is right, what God requires, what he asks. A pair of turtledoves or two young pigeons. The sacrifice of the poor. That is what we will offer for the Son of God. We cannot afford a lamb to die in his place.

Joseph buys the birds. And I hear footsteps echoing on stone. Jesus stirs in my arms.

And I see him, this old man who approaches me. His step is quick, his eyes alight. His hands reach for the babe I hold. His gaze touches mine.

And I see the question there. *May I? May I hold the Holy One?*

The man says his name is Simeon. And I realize I have heard of him before, a man righteous and devout, waiting for the consolation of Israel. It is he to whom it is said that the Holy Spirit has spoken — has told him that he will not see death before he has seen the Lord's Christ. In him I see all of us, all who have waited for the Promise, who have believed, who have hoped. Simeon represents faithful Israel. And just as the Spirit promised, in this moment the promise is fulfilled. To us all.

So I release my child. For the first time, I let him go and

place him in the arms of Israel. I give him, for this moment, to my people. What will my son find there? And what will Simeon see?

I let go, and the old man's hands shake as he takes the babe. He holds him close. Joy shimmers across his features as he turns his face to heaven. And he speaks. He prays:

> Now release your servant in peace, Lord, according to your word.

God has spoken. God will fulfill. Before my eyes God is doing as he promised one old man, as he promised all of his people.

> For my eyes saw your salvation
> which you prepared before the presence of all peoples.
> A light for revelation to the Gentiles . . .

The Gentiles. He mentions them first. The outsiders. The ones who have oppressed us.

> . . . and glory to your people Israel.

Glory? Glory! My heart fills with the promise. But what does it mean? I marvel at the words. Beside me Joseph marvels as well. Sometimes I cannot comprehend the vastness, the wonder, of what this child means. Sometimes I simply stand in awe, silent.

But this Simeon, this harbinger of the Spirit, is not finished yet. He turns to us and blesses us. And then his eyes fall on me. Just me. And he speaks of a strange kind of glory.

> Look! This child is destined for the fall and rising of many in Israel,
> and to be a sign that is opposed.

A sign? A sign of what? Why would he be opposed? Opposed? What kind of glory is that? I understand rising.

But must we fall as well? Lord, who will rise and who will fall? Will my son rise? Will he fall? Will I fall? What of my hopes, my dreams, my expectations? Will they fall too? I am not ready. I don't understand what it means ...

As if in answer, Simeon's eyes pierce mine. He looks deep into me. And suddenly the old man fades and I see a glimmer of an angel who called me favored, a gleam of a relative who called me blessed. I see the reflection of God.

With the babe still held close to his chest, he speaks again. And I receive his blessing meant for me alone:

And a sword will pierce through your own soul also.

And so I know. I hear. I learn what it means to be favored, what it means to be blessed. Somehow the blessing is a soul-piercing sword. I am to be pierced. He has prophesied my pain. Strange words, frightening. *Oh, Lord, what kind of blessing is this?*

I barely hear his next words as he places the baby back in my arms. The tones mix with the heartbeat of my son, with the sound of his quiet grunting.

So that the thoughts of many hearts may be revealed.

What is he saying? That there is purpose to my piercing? That there is meaning in the coming pain? Maybe. But still I don't understand. Why must the sword pierce? I have kept the law. I have done what my God requires.

And yet the Spirit speaks. An old man blesses me with a prophecy of pain.

Lord, am I really supposed to suffer?

The Wonder of Suffering

A haunting question. A frightening one. Are we supposed to suffer? Is pain a part of our blessing from God? We don't think so. We approach it as if it's something strange, something foreign that sneaks past God's protection. We behave as if we think that if we just do what's right, God will reward us with a life of ease. Then we act as if hurt and difficulty and struggle prove either our sin or that God has turned away. We cry out:

Are we supposed to suffer? Is pain a part of our blessing from God?

> "What have I done to deserve this?"
> "Why is God punishing me?"
> "Why can't I just learn whatever it is he's trying to teach me, so I can move on?"

Or we say:

> "Has God forgotten me?"
> "If God is good, why is life so hard?"
> "Maybe God doesn't love me after all …"

But then, in the midst of the cries and queries, comes Simeon's song to Mary. As we approach the temple with soaring hopes, crashing doubts, and questions that will not be answered, we see a woman who is declared favored, a girl called most blessed. And we hear an old man's song. A song that sings in harmony, yet in counterpoint, to Mary's Magnificat (Luke 1:46–55):

Mary sings: "He has helped his servant Israel … just as he promised our ancestors" (1:54–55).

And Simeon sings: Yes, there will be glory for Israel, but first the Messiah will be a light to the Gentiles. The first will be last, the last will be first (2:32).

Mary sings: "He has brought down rulers from their thrones but has lifted up the humble" (1:52).

And Simeon sings: Yes, he will cause the rising and falling of many. Many *in Israel*. He will be opposed. Oh, Mary, it won't look anything like you expect (2:34).

Mary sings: "He has scattered those who are proud in their inmost thoughts" (1:51).

And Simeon sings: "So ... the thoughts of many hearts will be revealed" (2:35). Not only the proud will be scattered. Not only the mighty will fall. He has come to reveal the hearts of all of us.

Mary sings: "From now on all generations will call me blessed" (1:48).

And Simeon sings: And that blessedness will be through the soul-piercing sword (2:35).

And as I listen to the song of Mary and Simeon, woven together in harmony, I find my world shaken, my suppositions exposed.

Maybe I'm wrong when I think the blessed life is the easy life.

Maybe I'm mistaken when I believe favor is when everything goes right.

Maybe God intends for my very soul to be pierced.

A startling concept. A scary peek into the intentions of the Spirit himself. Maybe pain is part of the plan.

A Friend's Divorce

I remember talking to a friend about this uncomfortable reality as she was going through a divorce. After twenty-five years of marriage, the counseling failed, the papers were filed, and her husband was spending his Christmas vacation with the other woman.

She was spending hers in tears.

So she sent me an email that went something like this:

I can't believe it hurts this much. Is it supposed to be this hard? He's out having a great time with his mistress, and here I sit, alone and crying. What did I do to deserve this? Why am I the one suffering? It's not fair. Is this what I get for loving him all these years? I never cheated. I never looked at another man. I was faithful. So why should I be the one crying every day while he has fun with his new girlfriend? I did what was right. I'm the one who deserves to be happy ...

Common thoughts, normal questions. Human ones. But these are questions that haven't grappled with the words of Simeon spoken to the woman whom an angel deemed "highly favored" and the one called "blessed."

Simeon, and the Spirit who speaks through him, calls us to wrestle with our view of blessedness and favor. What do we do with words like his? How do we incorporate them into a vision of a good God? How do we reconcile a soul-piercing sword with the idea of God's blessing?

How do we reconcile a soul-piercing sword with the idea of God's blessing?

Simeon did. Mary had to.

And so do we.

Even When Doing Right

Luke wanted to be perfectly clear about one thing: Mary was doing what was right, what was required by the law. "The framing story itself has one governing focus," says commentator Fred Craddock. "Jesus grew up in a family that meticulously observed the law of Moses. No fewer than five times in this text Luke tells the reader that they did everything required in the law." Four times Luke specifically wrote that what Mary and Joseph did in bringing Jesus to the temple was "according to the Law." Mary did everything she knew to do in order to obey God by bringing her son to the temple. She studied, she paid attention, she obeyed.

But then an old man approached. Not just any man, but one who was known for his goodness, his righteousness. Luke made sure we would know that the Spirit was on this man. Three times in three successive verses, Luke talked about the Spirit in connection with Simeon:

> "The Holy Spirit was on him" (2:25).
> "It had been revealed to him by the Holy Spirit" (2:26).
> "Moved by the Spirit" (2:27).

Just as the angel Gabriel spoke for God, just as Elizabeth was filled with the Holy Spirit (1:41), so now Simeon was speaking for God—a voice to be trusted, without doubt, without question.

Mary allowed Simeon to take the babe in his arms. She recognized the Spirit. And the old man prayed a beautiful, wondrous prayer of thanksgiving to God about fulfillment of promise and glory to Israel. How her soul must have soared! Luke said that she marveled, was amazed, at what Simeon said about Jesus.

But then came a shift. Simeon ended his prayer—his song of praise directed at God—and blessed the couple. Then he turned to talk directly to Mary. It's strange enough that he ignored the husband to speak only to the wife, but what he said is stranger still.

Blessings of Woe

With the air of "blessing" still on his words, Simeon gave Mary three successive "blessings" of woe that began with a wide, general focus and, with each step, narrowed to a more specific and personal pain.

First, he focused on the nation: Many in Israel would fall because of Jesus. And some would rise. There would be division. "Standing in the midst of the temple, the most splendid building imaginable, resplendent with gold and marble and alabaster, Simeon predicted that this baby would divide the people who built and loved that very temple," says commentator Bruce Larson.

The focus then narrowed to Mary's son: her son would not be welcomed but opposed. In contrast to the symbol of a righteous Simeon holding the Savior close to his bosom, Israel would not do the same. The Messiah himself, the one they had been waiting for, would not be embraced but rejected. Israel would not accept their King.

Finally, Simeon attuned his "blessing" tightly into Mary's very own soul: a sword would pierce through her inner being.

"I consider [these] words to be a turning point in Mary's life," says New Testament scholar Scot McKnight. "Simeon's words opened up a foreboding future ... Simeon announced that the future king's glory would come through sorrow and suffering." In other words, Simeon's song explained what Mary's song really meant. And it married, for the first time, the concepts of favor and blessing with the experience of deep inner pain and sorrow.

It is into that dichotomy that we must step if we are to understand the true character of God and what it means to be blessed by him. We must see a woman who began this journey with the words of surrender "Let it be to me as you have said," and who did all she knew that was right yet was told that despite it all she would receive the thrust of the soul-piercing sword.

She would experience piercing pain. Not because she was wrong, not because of sin, not because she deserved it, and not because God was punishing her. The sword would cut simply because she was meant to suffer too.

She was meant to suffer with her son. Simeon said that because Jesus would be opposed, because the consolation of Israel would not be embraced, pain would become a part of the blessing of being near Jesus. As he suffered, so would Mary. And so do we.

So That ...

And yet ... Simeon was not finished. His blessing did not end with the sword. Instead, with a single, small word, he gave us new vision and a new hope. "A sword will pierce your own soul," he said, "*so that* ..." In the Greek, it's a tiny conjunction: *hopos*. Most simply it means "in order that." But in reality, it means so much more. It means that everything Simeon had spoken of—division, opposition, and the piercing of the soul—wouldn't happen for nothing. The pain would have purpose; the suffering, meaning. Mary was called to suffer not for suffering's sake but for a purpose —for revelation. "So that the thoughts from many hearts will be *revealed,*" Simeon said, using the same word that appeared just a few verses above when he sang that Jesus would be a light of *revelation* (Greek, *apocalypto*) to the Gentiles. Revelation here means something we cannot know unless God himself shows us. We can't see it unless he pulls back the curtain with his own hand. This is a seeing, an understanding, that comes through the work of God himself, God alone.

> *We are meant to struggle. We are blessed with suffering. We are called to be like Jesus.*

According to the Spirit's words through Simeon, revelation comes through suffering, through the sword that pierces all the way to the soul. Through suffering the thoughts of our hearts are revealed. Through suffering we see the hand of God.

Our souls are laid bare in our suffering.

And that's the way it's supposed to be.

There is purpose in the pain.

So was Mary intended to suffer? Are you? Am I? Simeon said yes. It is part of walking with God, being his. Falling, rising, division, opposition, rejection, piercing pain … leading to revelation.

Because the promise of the coming Messiah has been fulfilled, favor and blessing now must include the soul-piercing sword. God has redefined favor. He has introduced a new type of blessing.

Yes, we are meant to struggle. We are favored with sorrow. We are blessed with suffering. We are called to be like him. Life is not intended to be easy. It never was.

Who Is This God?

Who is this God who calls us to a path we don't want to travel? Who calls us to sword and pain? Who made us to be like him?

He is the God of the soul-piercing sword. The one who suffers. He is the God who says through the apostle Peter:

- "Dear friends, do not be surprised at the fiery ordeal that has come on you to test you, as though something strange were happening to you." (1 Peter 4:12)
- "Even if you should suffer for what is right, you are blessed. 'Do not fear their threats; do not be frightened.'" (1 Peter 3:14)

And through the apostle Paul:

- "Not only so, but we also glory in our sufferings, because we know that suffering produces perseverance; perseverance, character; and character, hope." (Rom. 5:3–4)
- "Now if we are children, then we are heirs—heirs of God and co-heirs with Christ, if indeed we share in his sufferings in order that we may also share in his glory. I consider that our present sufferings are not worth comparing with the glory that will be revealed in us." (Rom. 8:17–18)
- "For it has been granted to you on behalf of Christ not only to believe in him, but also to suffer for him, since you are going through the same struggle you saw I had, and now hear that I still have." (Phil. 1:29–30)
- "Join with me in suffering, like a good soldier of Christ Jesus." (2 Tim. 2:3)

Because we are called, we are commissioned to be like him. And Luke tells us, "Did not the Messiah have to suffer these things and then enter his glory?" (Luke 24:26).

And this is just a small sampling of verses. I could add dozens more. So what do we do when we do right and yet suffer? When we surrender to God's will, when we follow his plan, when we read and study and pray and submit, and yet …

Then we do as Peter tells us: "Those who suffer according to God's will should commit themselves to their faithful Creator and continue to do good" (1 Peter 4:19).

Because the life of favor, the life of blessing, is also the life of the pierced soul. Because our God is the God who was pierced. This is the God of:

- *A righteous man* who was called God's servant, of whom God himself said, "There is no one on earth like him; he is blameless and upright, a man who fears God and shuns evil" (Job 1:8). And yet he lost his ten children in one day, not to mention everything he owned—his oxen, donkeys, sheep, camels, and servants. Then he lost his health. Boils sprung up all over his body, and at last he sat on an ash heap, scratching his sores with broken pottery and wishing he was never born. But he would encounter God speaking to him face-to-face in a whirlwind. Our God is the God of Job.

- *A prince* who was called a friend of the almighty God (Ex. 33:11), yet he wandered in the wilderness for forty years accompanied by people who complained and argued and made his life miserable. And he was not allowed to enter the Promised Land. But this man would speak to God face-to-face until his countenance glowed. Our God is the God of Moses.

- *A king*, whom God called "a man after my own heart" (Acts 13:22), yet fled for his life for years and was hunted, desperate, penning the words, "How long, LORD? Will you forget me forever? How long will you hide your face from me? How long must I wrestle with my thoughts and day after day have sorrow in my heart? How long will my enemy triumph over me?" (Ps. 13:1–2). But God would make with him an everlasting covenant. In his last words, he would call himself "the man exalted by the Most High" (2 Sam. 23:1). Our God is the God of David.

- *A God-Man*, called the Son of God, beaten, battered, bruised, whipped, rejected, mocked, and hung naked on a Roman cross to die. But he would rise again on the third day. Our God is the one who suffers …

This is our God, who sends Simeon to sing into our lives. To tell us that blessedness is not about ease but about reordering our very souls with a sword that cuts through all superficiality to what lies in the depths of each of us. It is about the falling and rising of many things in our lives. The things we thought mighty and important fall. The things we thought weak or insignificant rise. Our very selves are laid bare and then reordered, remade, by him.

That is the sword of blessing. That is the blade of favor.

So, take him into your arms. Gaze into his wonderful face. And let the sword do its work. There is no blessing without pain. There is no favor free from suffering.

Your life is not meant to be easy.

Embrace him ... and bare your very being.

You are favored. You are blessed. And a sword will pierce your soul.

CHAPTER 7

Running in the Dark
The Trip to Egypt

MATTHEW 2:13 – 15

There is a moment when all is well, when stars shine and the heavens sing with beauty. There is a moment when truth is celebrated, wonder is embraced, gifts are given. There is a moment ... and then the moment is gone. At that time, I realize the glimpse of glory was not meant to stay or be settled in. It was never meant to become a comfortable place where change is kept at bay. The glory was not an end but a means, a prelude, a preparation, to something more, something other than wondrous. It is the precursor to exile, to a flight in the dark, to a distant country where nothing is familiar and promises seem far away.

I have taken this strange journey, and so has Mary. A journey to a place that seems distant from all the dreams, all the hopes, all the promises God ever made. A journey to Egypt.

What do we do when God himself sends us away from everything we hoped for? What do we do on the road away from the Promised Land, when God seems distant, far behind us? And what does it mean to keep our faith when running in the dark, running scared?

Mary must have wrestled with these questions as she fled Israel with a babe in her arms and Joseph at her side. She must have struggled and wondered, with the threat of Herod chasing at her heels. Did she tremble in fear? Did she doubt? Did she question why God was sending her, and her son, away from the very people, the very land, who held the promises of a Messiah? What was it like to run in the dark and leave everything she knew behind her?

It may have felt something like this:

Mary Tells Her Story

He shakes me awake, and I stare up at eyes in the darkness. Wide eyes. Round. Fearful. It takes a lot to worry Joseph. But he is worried now. More than worried. Afraid.

Jesus? My gaze darts to the babe wrapped in blankets. Joseph has replaced the manger with a real crib, hewn from clean-smelling wood. Jesus sleeps there now. He sleeps soundly. I hear his baby grunts, though I cannot see him in the dark.

Joseph shakes me again. Gently but urgently. "We must go, Mary." His words leap at me in a frantic whisper. "Gather everything you can. Hurry!"

I throw back my coverings and jump to my feet. "What's happened?" I don't smell fire. I don't hear screams. I don't even hear footsteps. In fact, I hear nothing but the baby's quick breaths and Joseph's harsh ones.

"An angel, in a dream. He came to me. Warned me."

"What did he say?"

For a second, he doesn't answer. Then he turns his head toward the window, toward the west. "Rise, take the child and his mother, and flee to Egypt."

Flee? Now? Just when all is finally good? And to Egypt? So far ... so far from, well, everything.

"How long?"

His eyes come back to capture mine in the shadows. "He said, 'And remain there until I tell you.'" He pauses, his face shining dully in the moonlight. "Mary, he told me ..." He stops again. It's as if he cannot bear the next words. He closes his eyes.

I cannot close mine. "What did he say, Joseph? What else?"

"Herod is about to search for the child." He shivers. "To destroy him."

Herod. Chills race over my skin too, chills not from the night air but from the name that hovers between us. *Herod.* The one who calls himself king of the Jews, though he is no Jew. The one who killed his own wife, Mariamne, and his own sons when he thought they were plotting against him. The same one who has ordered that two thousand of our leaders be killed at his death just so there will be mourning. Herod, who would not hesitate to kill a baby in blankets to protect his throne. Wouldn't hesitate to kill a whole village of babes.

Would he?

I stumble toward my son. Evil now knows of this child. Herod knows of his rival, the true King of the Jews. The truth hisses through me. He knows ... and so he comes.

Oh, Lord ...

I grab a spare blanket and begin to throw in bread and dried figs. I grasp a jug for water and add our bit of olive oil to the pile. Joseph's tools, the baby's rattle. Seconds it takes to grab only what we will need. We will leave the rest. We will leave the new bowls that I've used but once. We will leave the half-finished table, the perfectly formed crib that has replaced a manger, the cozy room that has become a home. Everything that makes life easy. We leave it all.

But the gifts ... we take the gifts.

And then I lift my son, my little boy, who grunts in his sleep and turns in my arms. I take him and we run. In the night, in the dark, with only scant moonlight lighting our way.

Quickly, quickly.

Running scared.

In the dark.

In the night.

Leaving home behind.

The gifts jangle at Joseph's waist, and I remember. I remember Persian faces at my door. I remember men of a foreign court coming with the light of a star shining from their countenances. I remember them bowing before a baby, their foreheads touching the ground, just in the way Eastern peoples pay homage to a king. They came like the Gentile queen of Sheba to Solomon. And like her, they offered their gifts to the king.

Gold ... a precious gift to crown a king.

Frankincense ... incense to honor the divine.

Myrrh ... spice for burial.

Burial? Oh, Lord, was the gift a sign of things to come? Surely my son will not die ...

I force the question, the doubt, away. I focus on the wonder of the magis' coming. They knelt and worshiped, and I marveled. The world came to honor the King. The kings of the world came to his door ... so like David's son.

Like the promise, the dream, the hope of us all.

He is David's son.

How did that moment lead to this one? How did we come to this so quickly? For a single hour, it seemed, the world came to him, and believed. For just that short expanse of time, all was as it should be.

And then ...

And now ...

I stumble once as we run out of the village into the wilderness. Jesus jostles in my arms. He awakes. Cries. Then settles back to sleep.

He sleeps while our comfortable little world is torn apart by Herod's squall. He sleeps through the waves and wind of my running over uneven ground. He sleeps while I fight my way across a wilderness away from my people toward a land ruled by Gentiles. He sleeps through our great danger with his head cushioned on my breast.

He sleeps.

My gaze draws upward, to the sliver of moon that dips behind a cloud, to the stars that refuse to guide us as they did for the dignitaries of Persia.

"Lord, don't you care?" The words come to me from somewhere beyond my own fear. They echo to me from afar, settle in my soul. And I glance down at the sleeping babe.

Don't you care ...

That I run in the dark?

That a false king is coming to kill you?

That we flee to the land of slavery?

That we are leaving the promises behind?

I hold him tighter as I run. *Lord, save us! We're going to drown ...*

Drown in the madness of a king.

Eighty miles to Egypt. And then the harder journey across it to Alexandria, where they say at least a million Jews have made their home.

And I see. I understand. Just a bit, a tiny glimpse. Just as Jacob and his family fled to Egypt to save their lives, so we flee. Just as Moses was saved from a killer of infants by the waters of the Nile, so, too, will God save Jesus by the western edge of the Nile Delta. God will protect us. He will save his Son ... for now.

Egypt will welcome us. It welcomes the refugee. We will be safe.

But I am still afraid. Egypt may welcome us, but stay too long, and it will make you a slave. How could God be sending us so far away from the promises? How could he be sending us to exile?

The Wonder of Exile

Oh, Lord, how could exile be part of your plan? My own heart echoes Mary's cry as I imagine them fleeing back across a wilderness traversed by their ancestors, as I envision a dark flight to the land that once signified their slavery. I can scarcely grasp it — a dream, an angel, a midnight flight, a murderous king — such strange repercussions of a visit from foreign dignitaries bearing gifts. When the magi bowed before the child and opened packs to reveal the glitter of gold, the fragrant warmth of frankincense, the sweet bitterness of myrrh, Mary could not have known that their coming would set into motion events that would send her and her family running in the night to Egypt.

The Meaning of the Gifts

How wondrous it must have been to have Persian astrologers bowing down to her babe, bringing gifts she had never before seen or held in her hands — gifts far beyond her socioeconomic status. She and Joseph were poor, so poor they had to buy turtledoves in the temple because they could not afford a lamb. Yet here were gifts fit for a king. Finally, gifts that acknowledged who Jesus truly was.

I imagine how she might have held them, gazed at them, and perhaps believed that finally the promises of the angel, the hints of Elizabeth, the expectations of her own Magnificat, were coming true. She must have believed that it was finally all beginning—the hopes, the dreams, the victory—now that the world was coming to his door to honor him.

Remember how the queen of Sheba brought Solomon spices, gold, and precious stones. Remember how all the kings and queens of the world came to him and honored him for his wisdom. Remember how he built God's temple and filled it with the riches of all the world.

How could she not remember? How could she not believe that the magi with their gifts were but the first step on Jesus' journey to be Messiah-King? And how could she not remember all the hopes she had when she sang her Magnificat, and think that the gifts marked the beginning of all that was to be?

She was so wrong.

She was so right.

Because the coming of the magi was indeed the beginning of the Messiah's journey. But what a journey! Their arrival set into motion events that would lead not from gifts to glory but would instead take the Holy Family on a midnight flight to exile in Egypt. Their coming would not lead to Herod's throne but eventually to a Roman cross and a borrowed tomb.

> *God's goal is not safety, or comfort, or the simple path to glory. God values something else. And so must we.*

For Herod would only be the first to seek to kill the Christ. And his murderous rage was ignited not by anything Mary, Joseph, or Jesus did but rather by the simple visit of foreign men following a star.

But God sent the star anyway.

He sent a moment of glory that would end in a moment of flight, a moment of fear. And in that truth, we learn something significant about God. We learn, as Mary did, that God's goal is not safety, or comfort, or the simple path to glory. God values something else entirely.

And so must we.

A Fuller Perspective

But to see it, we need to step back and envision the world of that day with a wide-angle lens and picture the family as tiny players on a large map. From that perspective, we see dignitaries coming from the east—from Persia, which was considered the far eastern edge of their world. Then we see Mary, Joseph, and Jesus fleeing to the west, most likely to Alexandria, where Philo reports there were a million other Jews living at the time. Alexandria was at the far western edge of Egypt, the western edge of their world. From the far east to the far west, in the fullness of that journey, we glimpse the priorities of God—a Messiah not just for Israel but for the world, to the world.

The honor paid by the magi, the giving of kingly gifts, the wonder of dignitaries bowing to a babe in a cradle—none of it was about Mary's comfort, Mary's honor, Mary's safety and tranquility in Israel. It wasn't about the family being better off, having to struggle less, being able to settle in with a bit of security. It wasn't about any of the things we tend to value and ask for from God. Instead, God's priorities then were the same as they are now—that the world will encounter its Savior.

The Purpose of the Gifts

So, what was the point of the gifts? Why give them at all? Most scholars believe that the family used the magis' gifts to make their way to Egypt. In that way, the gifts became tools to make possible the family's flight. Their purpose was so that the family could go into exile.

It is at this point I must pause, ponder ... tremble.

The wondrous gifts that Mary held in her hands, that were so beyond anything she'd ever held before, maybe ever even imagined, the gifts that she would have treasured, were not to be hung on to, were not to be held tightly.

They would not bring her glory. They would not bring her wealth. They would not even be used to usher Jesus into his earthly kingdom.

They would be used to send Mary's family into exile.

And exile would save them.

This simple fact turns my world upside down.

What does this mean for the gifts God lavishes on me?

A Flight to Exile

And then, as if to emphasize the urgency of the exile, within one verse of the magis' departure, the angel appeared to Joseph in a dream. He told Joseph to take Mary and the child and flee to Egypt. No comfortable schedule, no advanced planning, just "Get up and run!"

The angel told Joseph what he needed to know when he needed to know it.

The way Matthew constructed this section of the story underscores what is important in it. To show Joseph's precise obedience, Matthew used the same words both in the angel's command and in Joseph's subsequent actions. The angel said, "Rise, take the child and his mother, and flee to Egypt." And Joseph "rose and took the child and his mother by night and departed to Egypt" (vv. 13–14, translation mine). Notice how Matthew slipped in the simple "by night" to show the immediacy of the flight—right on the heels of the magi's departure and the angel's command. Then Matthew changed but one word from the angel's command to Joseph's subsequent actions. The angel said to "flee." Matthew said they "departed." They left.

Why change that single word? I think it is meant to emphasize all they would leave behind. New Testament scholar Craig Keener sees it this way: "Jesus and his family survived, but they survived as refugees, abandoning any livelihood Joseph may have developed in

Bethlehem and undoubtedly traveling lightly.... Many Judeans had traditionally regarded refuge in Egypt as a last resort."

And so they went. Running scared, running in the dark, fleeing, leaving everything they knew behind them. In the middle of the night, they left the Promised Land. They went into exile. Because God himself sent them there.

So I must stop and wrestle again. God sent Mary, the favored one, into exile. She had done nothing wrong. She had surrendered. She had committed her life to God. She had obeyed at every step. And yet in the dark of night he drove her across a wilderness away from his people, his promises, and the temple where she worshiped.

> *Exile is part of God's purpose, part of his plan. Really?*

Exile is part of God's purpose, part of his plan. *Really?*

And for how long? For a day, for a month, for a year, for a decade? Mary didn't know. And neither do we. It could have been just for a short time, or it could have been for a couple years. The angel didn't specify for how long; all he said was, "Stay there until I tell you" (v. 13). No specifics, no reassurances, no "It'll be okay; it's just for a little while."

Mary was to stay in exile, far from all that had been promised, until God said to return.

She had to wait in faith far from home.

THAT IS GOD'S WILL.

For Mary. For you. For me.

Exile Is Not Forever

Yet there was hope. There was this subtle promise, this tiny glow in the angel's words. "Until I tell you," the angel said.

And so Mary knew, and we know, too, that exile is not forever. God will speak to us there. He is with us. He will call us home.

Then, like a mirror to Moses' return to Egypt from the wilderness, the angel again appeared to Joseph. In Exodus 4:19, the

Lord said to Moses, "Go back to Egypt, for all those who wanted to kill you are dead." In Matthew 2:20, the angel said, "Get up, take the child and his mother and go to the land of Israel, for those who were trying to take the child's life are dead." Moses returned to Egypt to set his people free, to lead them out of slavery to the Promised Land. Jesus returned to Israel to do the same.

Jesus returned at the earliest possible moment. Mary was called back from exile as soon as the threat was over. They were not sent there for no reason. They were not left there without cause. And the stay was not forever. "Like Israel, the child will return from exile and bring a new hope with him," says commentator Grant Osborne. Because those who wanted to kill him were dead. That which would have destroyed them had been defeated. Now was the right moment for return. Not sooner. Not later. Now. Osborne goes on to add: "The Davidic 'Branch,' both Messiah and Savior, has arrived, and as God saved him from Herod, so he will save us in the final analysis from all the evil that has turned against us. Jesus' return from Egypt is a promise to the church down through the ages that God ultimately delivers his people.... It was true with Jesus, it has been true throughout church history, and it is true now."

My Story ... and Yours

It is true for us all. This strange journey, this pattern from glory to exile to return, is not unique to Mary. I have seen it in my life. Perhaps you've seen it in yours. Because Mary's journey is our journey. Her God is our God.

> *This strange journey, this pattern from glory to exile to return, is not unique to Mary.*

So, as I wrestle with the unsettling juxtaposition of the wondrous visit of wise men with the horrifying threats of Herod, and see at the center a midnight flight, a young family running scared in the dark, I think—yes, I've been there—in the crosshairs of soaring hope and crashing fear, of everything-is-right and everything-is-wrong. I've been there, running in the wilderness, feeling as if God has driven me far from hope. I've been there with gifts that must be used in ways I never wanted to use them, in places I've never wanted to go.

- I've been to the mountaintop with gifts I thought would be mine forever, gifts that stunned me with their beauty.
- I've run through the wilderness in the dark of night with fear nipping at my heels.
- I've been in exile in my own Egypt when God seemed far away and hope a distant memory.
- I've seen the death of my Herods before I could be called home.
- And I've seen return when I realize that exile is not without purpose and I am not sent away forever. He brings me back, and hope with me.

The Mountaintop of Gifts

Just like Mary, my journey to Egypt started with a wonderful gift, one I had never seen before, one I could never afford. After months that had turned to years of failure after failure, the impossible had come true. I was pregnant after years of infertility. And with that gift came the smaller gifts of saltine crackers and soda water, a toy rattle bought in hope, a tiny outfit with a yellow giraffe, and a baby book where I pasted the positive pregnancy test. Like Mary, I received wondrous gifts from a place that had been so foreign, so distant. And like her, I held them in hands that trembled with awe.

I thought, *It's all coming true. Everything I've hoped, everything I've dreamed.* Finally, God was answering and things would be as they ought to be.

Joy. Wonder. Blessing. Beauty. I embraced it all. But this gift from God was not to be for my ease, my comfort. Instead, it sent me to exile.

Through the Wilderness

A dream came in the middle of the night, a strange dream of blood and cramps and pain. A dream of death. I woke, sweating.

And the next day, the dream came true. I started to bleed. I ran to the doctor's office.

I stumbled down the corridor, in the dark of a metaphorical night, with death hunting me, hissing thoughts of fear.

I've come for your baby.

And it had.

I lay there in the tiny room, watching the grey fuzz on the ultrasound monitor, listening to the doctor tell me how sorry she was, hearing the voice of all my fears—the dangers of bleeding out, the agony of the baby's loss, the ache of not knowing if we'd ever be able to have a baby again.

All the pain, all the grief, all the horrors of miscarriage.

Exile

I walked out of that doctor's office into a wilderness of doubts and fears, grief and confusion. I walked out with the gift of my pregnancy spent in a way I would not understand for many years to come.

> *I see now that the journey to a far-off country was not punishment but protection.*

And so I traveled to the far-off country of infertility treatments, schedules lined with monthly cycles, prayers unanswered, failure, slavery to a schedule made by doctors and month after month of disappointments and tears. A journey to a place where God seemed distant, his promises left behind on the shores of another land.

I was an exile, a foreigner in a foreign land.

What I didn't know, what I didn't see until later, was that God himself came with me. He traveled in my arms. And he changed me.

I see now that the journey to a far-off country was not punishment but protection. It was the place of transformation. I would see him in ways I never could have otherwise. I would see a God who is not interested in my ease and comfort but in making me the woman he created me to be. And he would do it in exile.

Herod's Death

Because while I was there, he would kill my Herods — my belief that his love could be measured by my happiness, that sorrow is caused by sin. He killed in me the expectation of a pain-free life. And he showed me how to use the gift of a pregnancy-gone-wrong to show others the love of a Savior in the midst of their own wilderness journey, their own exile.

He didn't allow me to cling to the gifts. Nor did he allow them to be wasted. With them he sent me into exile and there revealed the Messiah.

I found God in a new way out there past the wilderness, in my Egypt. Like Mary, I learned:

- Obey now, don't wait.
- You don't have to see where you're going for God to lead the way.
- What you receive in the light, use in the dark.
- God does not leave you or forsake you, even in the far-off land.
- Danger is real, but God is with you.
- God will not leave you in Egypt forever. "Out of Egypt," he says, "I will call my son." I will call my daughter.

The Return

And when he called me back, with the Herods of my life defeated, dead, I returned to the promises with rejoicing ... and with more wisdom than I ever could have gained had I stayed in my Israel. My exile turned into my first book on infertility and miscarriage

(*Empty Womb, Aching Heart*), and the opportunity to talk to others and encourage them on the same journey. And only then, after the exile, after the lessons, after the book was begun, did I get pregnant again and have our first daughter.

The return had meaning because I had used the gifts in a far-off land, and I had seen my Messiah in a new way there.

So, when we cannot see, when we run in the dark, when the things of God seem so far away, Mary's journey to Egypt tells us that God is protecting us; he is with us in the far-off land, and redemption and return are to come. The flight to Egypt is a call to trust him for our future when we cannot see the way. When life seems strange and uncertain, in flight and confusion: obey. Trust God, do what he says—even if it means running in the dark. Even in exile.

Who Is This God?

And yet I don't think I'll ever fully understand this story of the wonder of wise men bearing gifts, followed by a fear-filled flight into a dark desert, into exile. I grapple with it, want to reject it. But I can't.

Why must it be this way? Why must there be fleeing into the night? Why must there be fear-filled journeys to far-off lands? Does God really send us away?

And amid the questions, I hear a whisper, a single word: *Yes*. And I begin to see, I begin to get a glimmer of truth through Mary's story and through mine.

He is the God of gifts.

He is the God of exile.

He is the God of restoration and return.

The God of Gifts

He is the God who gives us wondrous things that we can barely imagine. He gives gold to honor us, frankincense to fill our lives with the aroma of his love, myrrh to prepare us for the burial of our old selves.

Burial. Death.

Gifts come not so we can bask in dreams-come-true but to prepare us for a midnight flight to Egypt. Gifts are meant to help us on a journey to a land where we've never been. Gifts are to be used in the process of transforming us and bringing the Messiah to those who are far from him.

That's what it means that our God is the God of gifts.

The God of Exile

God could have protected Jesus, Mary, and Joseph in Israel. He could have simply brought about Herod's death sooner. But instead, he sent the family on a perilous trip to Egypt, fleeing for their lives in the middle of the night. And death swept in behind them, with the murder of the boys of Bethlehem. Ramah weeps for her children because they are no more, the Bible says. And I weep with her.

Why, God? Why the death, why the horror? It is more than I can bear. More than I can conceive. But in this world, there is evil, there is wrong. There's a pharaoh who orders the death of all the Hebrew babies in Egypt. There's a führer who orders the death of millions of Jews. There's a young man who bursts into a school and guns down twenty kindergarteners in Connecticut.

And then there's miscarriage and cancer, hurricanes and heart attacks. Car accidents and gang wars.

There is danger. There is pain. There is running in the dark, not seeing where we're going, with fear biting at our heels.

Way back in the fourth century, early church father John Chrysostom said in his Homily 8.2 on this portion of the gospel of Matthew:

> Similarly, you yourself need not be troubled if you are suffering countless dangers. Do not expect to be celebrated or crowned promptly for your troubles. Instead you may keep in mind the

long-suffering example of the mother of the Child, bearing all things nobly, knowing that such a fugitive life is consistent with the ordering of spiritual things. You are sharing the kind of labor Mary herself shared. So did the Magi. They both were willing to retire secretly in the humiliating role of fugitive.

The God of Restoration and Return

But there is also return, restoration. You will not be in exile forever. This is a path that many have taken before me, before you. Surprisingly, this path from gifts to exile to restoration is the will of God. For Mary, for me, for you, even for King David.

After David was honored by Samuel and received the gift of Samuel's anointing him to be king of Israel (note that Messiah means "Anointed One"), David didn't ascend to the glory of the throne. Instead, the journey to the throne would go through the wilderness. David would run in fear from the threat of a mad monarch, the murderous king Saul. He would live in caves and in exile from the promise he received.

> *The God of gifts prepares us for a wilderness journey. The God of restoration will someday call us back to the promises he has made to us.*

During this time, David wrote Psalms 7, 34, 52, 54, 56, 57, 59, 63, and 142. In the wilderness, he learned to be a man after God's own heart. He learned to be the kind of king who would seek God not only in plenty but in want. And eventually the mad king would die, and the anointed one would return from running, return from a far-off country. God would call him back to take the throne and be the king of Israel.

And David isn't the only one who had a triumphant return from exile.

- Israel went from a family of seventy to a nation of millions ... in exile.

- Moses went from a murderer of an Egyptian to the one God called to lead his people ... in the wilderness.
- Daniel became a man of integrity and prophecy ... in exile.
- Esther saved her people from mass murder ... in exile.
- John the Baptist became the forerunner to Christ himself ... in the wilderness.

The God of gifts prepares us for a wilderness journey to a far-off country where the God of restoration will someday call us back to the promises he has made to us.

So, in your flight through the wilderness, in your exile to a far-off land, hold Jesus close, use your gifts to bring the Messiah to others, obey, and trust him that he will call you back just as soon as Herod is dead.

CHAPTER 8

Not Why but Who

The Search for a Son

LUKE 2:41–50

O ne story. One simple story from Jesus' childhood. It's all we
have of his growing-up years. And this has to be that story?
This story of a mother's frantic search and a boy's staying behind
in Jerusalem? Really, God? The only story you give us of Jesus'
growing up is when he was giving his mom a near heart attack?

Every parent remembers the moment with agonizing clarity.
You turn to the child who was standing beside you a moment
before, and he's gone. Vanished. You call. No answer. And then you
panic. You sweat and scramble and search and shout. You tremble
with a terror like no other. Your child is lost. As a parent, it's the
thing we have nightmares about, the thing we guard against with
endless warnings to our kids and tiny toddler backpacks with long
leashes. We activate locator apps on smartphones, we grip small
hands in our tight ones, and we imagine a thousand horrors if
something should go wrong. And eventually it does.

And for those few minutes, we experience the worst fear of
our lives.

So, I find it immensely unsettling that the only story we have of Jesus' childhood is when he was lost in Jerusalem. Of course, from his point of view, he wasn't lost at all. But from Mary's, he was gone, and she didn't know where to find him. But her search didn't just take minutes as she sprinted through the aisles of a store. Instead, it took three days to find Jesus.

Three days.

A number that chills me, because it whispers of another three-day span. Three days of darkness, of death, of nightmares-come-true. Three days he was lost.

So why is this the only story God gives us of Jesus' growing-up years? Why did Jesus stay in Jerusalem? Why didn't he tell his mother where he was? Why did he allow such pain, such fearful agony? Why wasn't Mary's concern, her well-being, at the forefront of his mind? Why did he cause his mother such suffering?

And what is it about this particular incident that shows us God as we may not have seen him before?

Maybe there is an answer in the very "whys" that plague me.

Because Mary asked why too. It's a human question. And it's my question whenever I am afraid.

Why?

A question Jesus won't answer.

But he will respond.

And in his words I find a whole new world opening before my eyes. I find a doorway out of fear.

For Mary it must have happened something like this:

Mary Tells Her Story

"Jesus, Jesus!" I call his name, but I do not find him. I call again with no answer.

I hear the braying of donkeys, the clatter of wagons pulling off the road. I hear the laughter of children and the scrape and tussle of men making camp for the night.

But I do not hear my son.

Dozens of friends and relatives have made the trek with us to Jerusalem for the annual Passover feast. Just like Samuel's parents, Joseph, Jesus, and I come every year. This year we travel with a large group, filled with men mostly, and some children and other women. All men are required to gather in Jerusalem for the Passover feast. I could have stayed home, and Jesus could have, too, as he is just twelve now, hovering on the cusp of manhood, tiptoeing along the border of the boy he once was and the man he will become.

Oh, how I love that boy.

But the man? Who is the man he will be?

The question whispers through me, and I push it aside. We will know soon enough. But for now all I want is to find him so we can make camp for the night. It has been a good journey. With some two hundred thousand other pilgrims to the walled city, we celebrated the Feast of Unleavened Bread, rejoicing in how God rescued us from slavery in Egypt so long ago. For eight days, we remembered the goodness of God as he gave our ancestors the sign of the blood of the lamb on their doorposts and the angel of death passed over them. Beggars sat at the city gates, merchants lined the streets, the bleating of lambs and goats filled our ears. We laughed with friends, we ate, we danced, we worshiped and sacrificed. We remembered the wonder of our redeeming God.

And now we have spent a full day on the road leading back home. I've chatted with neighbors, shared stories with friends, enjoyed remembering the celebration of God's goodness to me, to all Israel. All day I've assumed Jesus is with our relatives, playing with the other children. And now, as we make camp for the night, I still hear them running, playing hide-and-seek, calling out to each other. A happy sound.

But I don't hear his voice among theirs.

"Jesus?" I drop back in our caravan and call for him again. I stop a group of children as they run among the wagons. A boy, his cousin, looks up at me. "Where is Jesus?" I ask.

The boy shrugs. "I haven't seen him."

"He's not been with you?"

"No."

Fear nibbles at the corners of my mind. I hurry to another group of children. He is not there. They have not seen him. I stop a final group. They shake their heads.

My heart beats faster. I hurry to Joseph as he helps his uncle tie a donkey to their wagon. He stops his conversation about Roman politics and the number of soldiers seen in the city. His hands grow quiet on the rope as I slide to a stop before him.

"Mary?" His brows furrow.

"It's Jesus. I can't find him."

His face tightens. He hands the rope to his uncle. "We will make a careful search."

I nod. That is my Joseph. Careful, thoughtful. As usual, he does not hesitate to do what he must to protect his son, to protect Jesus.

So we search ... among all the children, all our relatives, the wagons, the groups, the donkeys.

And we don't find him.

My hands shake. My heart thuds.

I grab Joseph's sleeve. "What are we going to do?"

"Jesus! Jesus!" I yell his name even though I know he can't hear. I know he's gone.

Joseph glances back along the road. "Back, back to Jerusalem."

So we run, back along the path, dust kicking behind us. We race toward Jerusalem, with fear at our heels. It seems I am always running with this child. Run to Elizabeth. Run to Egypt. Run back to Jerusalem. Too much running. Too much fear.

And as I run, I think of all the things that could have happened to him. I think of robbers on the road. Kidnappers. Slavers. He could have fallen in a well. He could be hurt. Is he crying for his mother? Is he looking for me and unable to find me? *Oh, Jesus ... I am coming, my son.*

Where are you?

And I pray as I run. Desperate prayers, fearful prayers. Short and staggering. Anguished.

I have lost my son.

We journeyed a day from Jerusalem. It takes us less than that to return. We don't find him on the road. We don't find him at the city's gate. So, we search the market. We hunt down the streets where we stayed. The bread booths, the fish stands, the pens now nearly empty of lambs and goats. We hear the soft bleating of those that remain. The sound echoes mournfully in my soul.

And still we do not find him.

Lost.

We look everywhere. Everywhere. All day we search and into the next. Has he been captured and sold? Has he been run down by horses, captured by soldiers, killed by a governor that holds the name of Herod?

A thousand scenarios. A thousand fears.

I have nearly given up hope. Three days. Lost for three long days, three eternities. He is gone. Will I never see him again?

Where is my son?

God, help me! Help me find him. Oh, God, I am so afraid ...

We go to the temple. Perhaps the priests will pray. Perhaps they will help us.

The scribes and teachers of the law are gathered in a tight group. I rush to them. "Help me, help me," I cry.

They part, and I see him. My son, my Jesus, sitting among them, listening and asking questions. Unharmed, unkidnapped. Safe.

Those around him are astonished at him. I am astonished, too, but not from his understanding, his observations.

He smiles at me.

I run to him. Again, I am running.

I cry and shout and weep and shake him.

"Why?" I cry out. "Son, why did you do this to us?" It is my one question, my only question. My "why" rings against the stones.

But he doesn't answer it.

I hold him close, then grip his shoulders and shake him again, gently, firmly. "Look," I say, "your father and I have been anxiously searching for you." Can he see the suffering in my face, the pain that must still etch my features? Doesn't he understand the torment he has caused me? Why? Why...?

He pulls back from me. He looks deep into my eyes.

My trembling ceases.

And he answers. He doesn't tell me why, but he answers all the same.

"Why were you searching for me? Didn't you know I had to be in my Father's house?"

I had called Joseph his father, but Jesus reminds me of a strange truth. He has another father. A true father. He is God's Son.

He looks at me, willing me to understand ... not *why* but *who*. Who he really is. Unlike any who have gone before him.

Unlike David, unlike Solomon, unlike *any* of the heroes of old, this one calls God "Father."

I don't understand. I can't. Not all of it.

Who is the boy not yet a man? Who is he who says of God, "my Father"? He is more than I ever dreamed … more than I can comprehend.

But there is something I see … a glimpse, a tiny, tiny peek, of who he really is.

Because one thing I do know: this son who has refused to answer my "why" has answered "who." He wants me to see him for who he truly is. He offers no explanations. Instead, he offers himself. And in this moment, I see — I have been asking the wrong question all along.

The Wonder of Who

I often speak about the God of Mary's journey at women's retreats and various conferences. I love talking about life in the barn, the transformation of the cross, the wonder of the resurrection. But this story? This strange pericope of panic and searching and accusation? Three sentences, and then I would hurry on to the next portion of Mary's journey. I didn't like to settle here. It was just too odd, too uncomfortable. After all, when I'd lost my just-turned-three-year-old son, Jayden, at Disneyland for three whole minutes, I thought my heart would explode from beating so hard. I didn't like to remember that feeling as we raced back to the restaurant to look for him. I didn't like to review all the what-ifs and could-haves. I didn't want to recall how my breath rushed through my lungs, how my palms became sweaty, how I envisioned the worst in those few minutes he was lost to me. And he was gone only three minutes, not three days. So I especially didn't want to consider how Jesus did that to his mom. I didn't want to look too closely at that!

But in the middle of one such speaking engagement, God nudged me. Well, it was more like a shove. There I was putting on my mascara, running through that day's talks in my mind, and trying not to jab myself in the eye with the mascara wand. I'd spoken about finding God in the most unlikely places. I'd talked about surrender and hope. I'd discussed the beauty of gifts given and songs sung in joy. Later I was planning on talking about Mary at the wedding in Cana. And I was diligently avoiding a discussion of the time Jesus gave his mom a panic attack.

I liked my plan.

God didn't.

So he poked me, spiritually speaking, of course. "Look at that childhood story again."

"No. It's weird. I can't see anything there."

"Look again."

"I know the story." And I did. I knew it was the only story in the whole Bible about Jesus' childhood. I knew it was the first time we hear Jesus speak in the Gospels.

And right there I should have realized that God had placed something essential in those words. I should have known that if I looked more carefully he would reveal something profound.

Then came the quiet whisper in my soul: *Don't you see, Marlo, that everything you need to say today is right here in this one story.*

"Huh?" was my oh-so-articulate response to God.

The question. Ponder Mary's question.

"Oh? Oh. Ohhhhhh ..."

And I saw.

Mary asked, "Why, God? Why are you treating me this way? Why did you do this to me?" Why? Why? Why? It's the question we all ask when life throws us a curve. How many times had I asked that exact same question?

Asking Why

God, why did you let our church plant fail? It was the first of many "whys." We'd poured our hearts and lives into starting a bicultural church in a "bad neighborhood" in the small city of Gilroy, California. We partnered with a bilingual pastor, we rented a small building off of Main Street, we bought a van (with our own money) to pick up kids around the poorer neighborhoods and bring them to church. I even took a position as a long-term substitute in bilingual math at the local high school (even though I don't speak Spanish—I learned numbers and math terms fast!). We loved that church. We loved the people. We loved the dream of sharing the love of Christ with people of all backgrounds.

But we didn't count on cultural differences driving a wedge between the bilingual pastor and the non-Hispanic members of the church. We didn't realize that people would fight over money, that bills would not be paid, and that founding members would sit on our couch in tears explaining why they couldn't keep on. And it wasn't their fault. The church was crumbling, and we couldn't resurrect it. Only God could. But he chose not to.

I will never forget how I cried as we drove away from that tiny building for the last time. I remember the little box of personal items in the backseat. I remember the way the vinyl sign hung crookedly in the storefront window. CORNERSTONE CHURCH OF THE NAZARENE in block letters, with the words *Piedra de la Iglesia del Nazareno* in script beneath. I remember the Bible clutched in my hand and the way my husband stared out the car's windshield and couldn't say a single word.

And I remember the question I asked: "Why, God, why did you treat us like this? Why did you let the vision fail? Why did everything we hoped for disintegrate before our eyes?" We had worked out of love for God and his people. We had sacrificed. We had done everything we knew how to do. But God still didn't show up and save the church.

Why?

I asked the same question when our two IVF (in vitro fertilization) cycles failed a few years later. "Why, God? Why won't you give children to us when we'll raise them in the love and knowledge of God? Why do you, instead, allow people to get pregnant who don't even want to be? Why do you give babies to women who abort them and none to me? Why do teens get pregnant after one night in the back of a Chevy, and my God-loving husband and I can't get pregnant at all? Why won't you give me a baby? Why won't you just say yes? Why is life so unfair? Why don't you love me enough?"

Why?

And in this simple pericope, God shows me that I have been asking the wrong question all along.

The Wrong Question

Just like with Mary, our own "whys" often start with something going wrong. Our expectations are shattered. Jesus isn't where we expect him to be. He seems absent. We can't find him.

So we search for Jesus. We search for God. In pain, in hurt, in fear, we look for God where we think he ought to be. He should be with the relatives, with friends, with acquaintances. He should be where he's always been.

He should answer our prayers.

But when he's not there, when our prayers are not answered in the way we hoped, then the fear, the worry, and the panic set in. We are like Mary rushing back to Jerusalem. "Where is Jesus in this mess?" we ask. "Why isn't he helping me? Why doesn't he fix this? Is God lost?" We are in pain, agony. And there is no easy fix from an all-powerful God. And that hurts. In verse 48, Mary describes her feelings with the

When our prayers are not answered in the way we hoped, then the fear, the worry, and the panic set in.

word *odynaomai*, a strong term meaning to cause great anxiety, anguish, mental distress, pain, and sorrow.

It is here that many commentators become uncomfortable and insist on including the word *unintentionally* or *unconsciously* when describing how Jesus caused his parents pain. I don't blame them. I am uncomfortable too. They cannot accept that Jesus *knowingly* caused Mary pain. After all, he was a good boy. Luke even ends this section by saying so: "Then he went down to Nazareth with them and was obedient to them" (v. 51). But does that mean he will not intentionally cause pain?

John Nolland thinks so. He says, "Jesus was genuinely surprised, and no doubt grieved that his parents had experienced such distress." R. Kent Hughes goes further, arguing, "The point is, he was capable of *unknowingly* causing his parents distress; but as a sinless being, he was incapable of *knowingly* doing it."

But is this true? Is it a sin to cause pain? Or, more precisely, is it sin to knowingly cause pain in order to follow God's will? And would Jesus, who embodies the character of God in human form, ever intentionally cause us pain?

We don't like to think so, but then what will we do with verses like these:

- "You [God] crushed us and made us a haunt for jackals; you covered us over with deep darkness." (Ps. 44:19)

- "Yet it was the LORD's will to crush him and cause him to suffer, and though the LORD makes his life an offering for sin, he will see his offspring and prolong his days, and the will of the LORD will prosper in his hand." (Isa. 53:10)

- "The LORD has rejected all the warriors in my midst; he has summoned an army against me to crush my young men. In his winepress the Lord has trampled Virgin Daughter Judah." (Lam. 1:15)

And what do we do with stories such as Jonah's, when God sent the worm to devour the plant that Jonah valued? Jonah was angry then, angry enough to die. Did God not cause his pain? What about Jeremiah, whom God called to prophesy in pain and tears? Or Hosea, whom God made to marry a faithless woman? Or Job, whom we'll talk about later in this chapter?

I could go on, but then there's Jesus himself. In his ministry, did he never cause his followers pain, fear? He did. He did things that would terrify them.

He told his followers that they would have to eat his flesh and drink his blood, which distressed so many that "from this time many of his disciples turned back and no longer followed him" (John 6:66).

He slept in the boat during a wild storm when the disciples thought they would die. They felt compelled to ask, "Teacher, don't you care if we drown?" (Mark 4:38).

He would walk on the lake toward them until they cried out in terror thinking he was a ghost (Matt. 14:25 – 26; Mark 6:47 – 50).

To keep us from pain, from fear, is not God's top priority. It wasn't Jesus' either. It still isn't.

So, what do we see from this incident from Jesus' childhood? That Jesus at age twelve was so clueless that he didn't realize his parents would worry? Or perhaps do we see that pain is an intentional result of not understanding who Jesus really is?

I think it's the latter. When God causes us pain, it's not an "oops" but rather an opportunity to encounter him more genuinely, to see him for who he truly is. God's purpose is that we might know him. His priority is not that we live pain-free.

This story tells us so.

We see it when Mary and Joseph finally found Jesus among the teachers at the temple. Mary's first words tell the story: "Son," she asked, "why have you treated us like this?" (v. 48). She did not say, "Oh, we're so

Mary knew, as we do, that it was in Jesus' power to prevent pain. And he didn't. He doesn't. Not always.

happy we found you. You must not have understood how worried we'd be." No, she asked what we all ask. "Hey, why did you do this to me?" She knew, as we do, that it was in Jesus' power to prevent pain. And he didn't. He doesn't. Not always.

So, pain happens, fear happens, agonizing anguish happens. And then we find him. And what do we do then? In our fear, in our frustration, and in our anger, we ask, "Why?" And we ask it so very like Mary: "God, why? Why did you put me through this? Why did you treat me like this? I thought you loved me. So why? Why, why, why?"

And Jesus doesn't answer that question.

Instead, he gives us a glimpse of who he is.

The Right Question

When Jesus responded to Mary (as he does to us), he made no excuses. He didn't say, "Oh, I'm so sorry, I didn't realize you would be hurt." Rather, he turned the "why" back on his mother: "Why were you searching for me?"

And he answered with another question: "Didn't you know I had to be in my Father's house?" (v. 49). In other words, "Don't you know who I am?" "So the first recorded words of Jesus are a statement about himself," says commentator Michael Wilcock.

And in Jesus' questions, he implied that if Mary had only seen him for who he truly is, she wouldn't have been afraid, she wouldn't have been searching anxiously, she wouldn't have had days filled with panicked pain. The problem was not that Jesus had vanished but that Mary hadn't grasped a basic truth about his identity.

Scot McKnight puts it this way: "In this question, Jesus revealed who he was: Jesus told Mary that God, the One God of Israel, was uniquely his Father." This is the first time anyone in the Bible has called God his individual, personal Father. In the Old Testament, God is referred to as "Father" only fourteen times, and in each time the word is used in reference to God being the father of Israel as a nation. But Jesus would call God his personal

Father here for the first time and never use any other term when addressing God. In fact, in the Gospels as a whole, we see Jesus calling God his Father a full sixty times. R. Kent Hughes says, "Jesus called the temple where he stood his 'Father's house,' and in doing so he asserted that God was his Father and that he stood in unique relationship to God—that he had a relationship to God that no other human has ever had."

So, Jesus said that Mary was not looking for him for the right reason. She wasn't looking because she wanted to see who he really was. She was simply afraid, confused, panicked at not finding him. And she couldn't find him because she was seeing him as Joseph's son, the one whom she expected to follow Joseph home from Jerusalem.

Her expectations were wrong. Her assumptions were based on an incomplete understanding of Jesus' identity. We see that faulty understanding most clearly when she asked the question "Why?" and named Joseph as Jesus' father. Jesus responded by showing her "who" and revealing that the God of the temple was his true Father. In doing so, he answered her fears, her frustrations, and her accusations not with explanations but with a glimpse of glory. He showed her a truth about himself that no one else had seen before. He showed her his uniqueness.

The angel had told her that Jesus would be called God's Son. But it was not until this incident when Jesus was twelve that Mary could begin to understand what that might mean. He is the Son of YHWH himself, the one who embodies the very nature and divinity of God. He is not just Messiah. Not just rescuer and ruler. He is the very Son of God.

And in that moment, Jesus revealed the wonder of who he is in a way that should have made Mary tremble in awe. But instead, she and Joseph didn't understand. We may not either. "The depths implicit in Jesus' identity as Son of God … are more than his human parents are yet able to fathom, and they are left puzzled," says Nolland.

I think they couldn't grasp it because they were asking the wrong question based on a wrong assumption based on an insufficient understanding of the true nature of Jesus. Not so different from you, or me. Mary was thinking of Jesus as Joseph's son, so she assumed he was with them in the caravan, and then when she discovered he had stayed behind in Jerusalem, she asked only "Why?" Our incomplete perception of Jesus will cause us to make wrong assumptions about him that result in our crying out to him, "Why, God? Why?"

But when we are focused on the "why," we cannot see all that God wants us to see. We are listening for "why," and he is answering "who." So we miss the glimpse into the wonder of who he really is. We miss the very thing that would assuage our fear, our doubt, and our difficulty, the very thing that God most wants to offer us — a deeper, clearer understanding of himself.

> *When focused on the "why," we cannot see all that God wants us to see. We are listening for "why," and he is answering "who."*

Must it be this way?

No.

We can change the pattern. We can ask the right question. What if the next time things go awry, when we can't see God, when we're afraid and running to and fro, we don't ask why? What if we don't cry, "Why is this happening to me?" or "Why are you treating me this way, God? Why won't you answer?" What if we ask instead, "Who are you, God, in this situation? Show me yourself in a deeper way. Give me a glimpse of *you*."

What if we ask, "Who?"

How would that change us? What then would we see, would we understand? After all, "Who?" is the question God longs to answer. He answers through a boy lost three days in Jerusalem. He answers it again through a man dead three days in a tomb. A boy found. God found. A man alive. God resurrected. By understanding this "who," we find healing. We discover wonder. We glimpse the breathtaking beauty of a vivid God who wants more than to assuage our fear.

He wants to show us himself.

Who Is This God?

This one small story that sits precariously between Jesus' infancy and adulthood, the only story we have of his childhood, does an amazing thing. It not only foreshadows Christ's death and resurrection, it also reflects the heart of the whole book of Job in a few brief sentences. In Job, my favorite book of the Bible, we see this strange dichotomy between our "why" and God's "who" stretched out into forty-two chapters. Most people hate to read Job. Most think it's a book about suffering.

But it's not.

It's about God being the God of "who" and not the God of "why." It's about being taught to ask the right question.

The book opens with a peek behind the curtain—a scene showing Satan presenting himself to God. Immediately, in chapter 1, the reader is shown why all kinds of tragedy will befall Job. Job is never told, never shown, what happens here behind the scenes. Only we know that God himself brings Job to Satan's attention. God brags about this righteous man who honors him. "Have you considered my servant Job?" God asks. "There is no one on earth like him; he is blameless and upright, a man who fears God and shuns evil" (Job 1:8).

Satan is not convinced. He says Job's righteousness is only a result of God's blessing. "But now stretch out your hand and strike everything he has, and he will surely curse you to your face," Satan counters (Job 1:11).

God allows Satan to take everything—all of his oxen, his donkeys, his servants, his sheep, his camels, and finally his children. Job mourns, but he does not curse God. Then God allows Satan to take even Job's health. Job sits on an ash heap scratching his wounds with a broken piece of pottery. He sits and scratches and wishes he were never born.

And still Job does not curse God.

But he does ask why. Five times in his opening soliloquy, he asks God, "Why?"

His friends, who had sat with him silently for seven days, are eager to offer their answers. For thirty-four long chapters, they attempt to explain to Job why God has done this to him. And for thirty-four long chapters, Job knows their answers are wrong. "You've sinned, you've done evil, you deserve this," they say. "I have not, I do not," Job replies. But still, like so many of us, he continues to cry out various poetic versions of "Good grief, what did I do to deserve this? God, why is this happening to me?"

Then, finally, in the midst of one of Job's friend's concluding argument for why God is too grand to show up, God shows up. God speaks out of the storm, the whirlwind.

The friends are silenced.

Job is silenced.

And God speaks. For four chapters.

In all those 129 verses, God gives not even a single hint to answer the question of why. He says nothing about the events of the first two chapters of Job. He gives Job no explanations at all. But in every single verse, he does answer another question. He answers, "who." In some of the most beautiful ancient poetry that we have, God paints an amazing, vivid picture of the wonder of the God of all the universe.

He says, here is who I am. I am the God who ...

- laid the earth's foundations (38:4)
- shut up the sea behind doors (38:8)
- gives orders to the morning (38:12)
- shows dawn its place (38:12)
- walks the recesses of the deep (38:16)

- sees the gates of deepest darkness (38:17)
- owns the storehouses of snow and hail (38:22–23)
- cuts a channel for the torrents of rain and a path for the thunderstorm (38:25)
- fathers the dew (38:28)
- births the frost (38:29)
- binds the chains of the Pleiades and loosens Orion's belt (38:31)
- brings forth the constellations in their seasons (38:32)
- wrote the laws of the heavens (38:33)
- covers himself with a flood (38:34)
- directs bolts of lightning (38:35)
- gives wisdom (38:36)
- hunts for the lioness (38:39)
- provides food for ravens (38:41)
- knows when the mountain goats give birth (39:1)
- watches the doe bear her fawn (39:1)
- frees the wild donkey (39:5)
- is served by the wild ox, who stays by my manger at night (39:9)
- gives speed to the ostrich (39:18)
- gives the horse its strength (39:19)
- gives the hawk flight and makes the eagle soar (39:26, 27)
- has a voice like thunder (40:9)
- is adorned with glory and splendor, clothed with honor and majesty (40:10)
- brings the proud low (40:11)
- tames Behemoth (40:19)
- makes a pet of Leviathan (41:5)
- and saves you because you cannot save yourself (40:14)

He says, I am more than you ever dreamed, more than you ever hoped, more than you can even imagine.

And Job puts his hand over his mouth. No more whys, no more questions, just the wonder of an awesome God. And Job is satisfied … because God never answered why, but God did show him who. God gave Job an incredible, amazing glimpse of a God who is so mighty and powerful and majestic that he created the earth and made the stars to sing, but is also so close and intimate and caring that he is there in the secret places where the doe gives birth, where the mountain goats bear their young. This one who tames the Behemoth and Leviathan can also tame our lives, our hearts. He is the Answer.

That's the gift Job is given in chapters 38–41: a glimpse of the wonder of God, the true answer to all questions. And it's our answer when life isn't fair, when our health is bad, when we grieve, when loss catches us by surprise, when the life we lead has lost its luster. The answer is the wonder of God, the reality of who he is.

All the answers to "why" will not satisfy the longing in our souls. But God's answer of "who" satisfies us with wonder.

All the answers to "why" will not satisfy the longing in our souls. They leave us empty. But God's answer, the answer of "who," fills us with glory, amazes us with magnificence, and satisfies us with wonder.

In C. S. Lewis's *Till We Have Faces*, the main character, Orual, says: "I know now, Lord, why you utter no answer. You are yourself the answer. Before your face questions die away. What other answer would suffice?"

He is the answer. He always has been.

Job discovered that. So did Mary. Will I? Will you? Will you stop asking why and instead discover the awesome who that is our God?

CHAPTER 9

The Fine Art of Waiting
Water and Wine

JOHN 2:1 – 11

W hat does wonder look like in the land of waiting? What if you go months, years, even decades, believing in God's power and promises but not seeing that power revealed in your circumstances? Mary had been there, in the waiting place. She believed the angel's words in Luke 1, she sang of what God would do in her Magnificat, but now decades had passed. Jesus had not stepped forward in power, had not revealed his majesty, had not conquered Rome. Then, tucked away at a wedding in Galilee, she heard those words again: "My hour has not yet come."

Nevertheless, a transformation was about to take place. Not only of water into wine but of Mary herself. From mother to follower. From parent to disciple.

So, as we wrestle with a God who asks us to wait, God is beckoning us to come to a wedding at Cana. As we struggle to understand a God who sometimes does not come through with the power we are looking for in the time frame we want, he is inviting us to come alongside Mary. As we question a God who sees the need and still says "not yet," he calls us to watch Mary touching the sleeve of her son. To hear her words, "They have no wine."

Let us wait with her. Because transformation will come. Of water. Of stone jars. Of need. Of worry. Of the waiting itself. Because we, too, will be transformed.

For Mary it happened something like this:

Mary Tells Her Story

Laughter swirls around me. Dancing and feasting and fun. I've come with my children to the wedding feast of my relative in Cana. It's a large feast that has been going on for days. But something is wrong. I sense it.

I see my son sitting with his disciples. He has disciples now, just a few, but followers all the same. And he's gone to the Jordan to be baptized by Elizabeth's son. They say something extraordinary happened there, but I didn't see it. All I know is that he vanished for forty days and came back looking like a skeleton. He still seems too thin to me, not like the boy I raised or the man who grew muscular at the carpenter's trade.

A few paltry disciples, that gauntness to his cheeks, hidden away here in Cana at Galilee. I sigh. I've waited years, decades, for him to become the man the angel promised, the one I once sang about, the one we have waited for since the days of the prophets of old.

Messiah.

Redeemer.

King.

He is to be all of these. So I've waited, I've wondered, I've hoped and prayed and wished and watched and . . .

And here we are. He doesn't seem like a messiah. He doesn't act like a redeemer. He certainly doesn't look like a king.

When, God? When will he be who I want him to be?

I hear the servants whispering. Their heads are close together, their hands fidgeting. One glances over at me.

"What is it?" I say.

One of the servants scuttles toward me. "We don't know what to do. It's terrible. It's ... it's just that ..."

A second servant sidles up. "Tell her."

"We've run out of wine."

My eyes widen. It is terrible. Tragic. The bridegroom and bride will be shamed, their marriage said to be doomed to sorrow. In our culture, wine is the symbol of joy. It is blessing. King David sang of it:

> Let the light of your face shine on us.
> Fill my heart with joy
> when their grain and new wine abound.

And his son, Solomon, wrote:

> Go, eat your food with gladness, and drink your wine with
> a joyful heart, for God has already approved what you do.

So, oh, we cannot run out of wine at the wedding feast! I glance at the young couple and bite my lip. Then I turn and look again at my son. I have learned to rely on him since Joseph died. He is my firstborn, the son who provides for his brothers, his sisters, and me.

Maybe there is something he can do now.

I go to him. He turns from his small group of followers and looks at me.

I hesitate. But I am his mother; I have a right to ask. "They have no wine."

A simple statement, and in it a million questions.

I don't even really know what I'm asking. Not fully. Do I

ask for a miracle? No, I have no reason to expect that. So do I want him to commiserate with me, to find a solution, to go buy wine?

I don't know. But I come to him anyway. I tell him the need. And I wait. I am good at waiting.

For a moment, he doesn't say a word.

Then he says one: "Woman."

It is not harsh, not demeaning, but it is not "Mother" either. It is not an endearment. He speaks as if I am just a woman, just another person at this marriage feast. Just a woman, and not the special one who gave him birth. Why does he not call me "Mom"?

Then he says more. He uses a phrase that shows me the distance between us. "What is this between you and me?" he asks. What does he mean by it? Does he ask why I should involve him? Doesn't he know? I involve him because he is my son. Are we at odds? Are we separate? What is he saying to me in that simple phrase?

He calls me "Woman." He does not submit to my request. And I see, yes, I see it now. He is asking something of me.

I have come to him as a mother to her son. But he is asking more.

Then he speaks words that pierce my very soul: "My hour has not yet come." *Hour.* He says the word in a way that makes me shiver. As if I might not like it when it does come. But how could I not? His *hour* ...

And suddenly I am remembering an old man in the temple, how his blessing of prophecy fulfilled became also a soul-piercing sword.

The words trample through my mind again. His hour. Still not come. Still ...

Then I see. He is willing me to see, to change. I thought I

The Fine Art of Waiting

was asking something of him, but he is asking something of me. He is asking that I be "woman," that I submit not to my timing but to his. He is asking me . . .

Oh . . .

So I let go. Of my questions, of my assumptions, of my demands.

I am not the parent here. *I am the disciple. I am the follower.*

That is what he is asking of me. He is asking me to trust him. Not only to meet a need but to do it in his own timing.

And I see the temple again, but this time I see a boy sitting in the midst of the teachers, calling God his very own Father.

This is God's Son. He will do as the Father wishes in the Father's time. Not mine.

I am called to wait. To watch. To submit. And to do whatever this Messiah-Son asks of me.

He will ask. I will obey.

I turn to the servants, and I am changed, transformed. "Do whatever he tells you," I say. And I leave it at that. I will speak no more.

I see it then, the tiny smile that brushes over his lips then is gone.

He knows. He knows I am changed.

But what will he do now?

He turns to the jars lining the wall. There are six stone water jars for our Jewish rites of purification; each holds twenty to thirty gallons of water. They are empty. As empty as the wine bottles. Everything we've relied on is gone.

I wait.

"Fill the jars with water," he says to the servants. Just that, nothing more.

I don't say a word.

The servants do as they are told. They do it in abundance.

They fill those jars right to the very top, to the brim. What do they expect that they fill them so full?

"Now draw some out and take it to the master of the feast," Jesus tells them.

A strange request, but I don't question it. I just watch. I wait. The Messiah is at work, and for now, for me, that is enough.

The servants draw out a cup full of water. It glimmers, and I gasp. It doesn't look clear. It looks ... it appears ... wine red.

They take the cup to the master of the banquet. He doesn't know where it came from. He can't know. But I do. The servants, his disciples, and I. A ragtag bunch we are, but we are the ones who know.

Jesus turns back to his followers. I see that same smile brush across his face, the smile that comes with transformation. First mine, and now the water's.

The master of the feast sips from the cup. His face changes. He calls to the bridegroom. He swirls the liquid in the cup then holds it up to the groom. "Everyone serves the good wine first, and when people have drunk freely, then the poor wine." He shakes his head and again drinks.

And that's when I know for sure. It is not water anymore. It is wine. Jesus has transformed it. Just as he transformed me.

"But you have kept the good wine until now."

The good wine.

I laugh. A miracle. His first. And it is a miracle of transformation. Not of power. Not of might. But simply changing water into the wine of joy. I did not expect a miracle, but I got one. But maybe it is not a miracle at all, rather a sign. A sign of what is to come with this Messiah who does not seem like a messiah. A Redeemer who does not act like a redeemer. A King who does not look like a king. This is the Messiah, Redeemer,

King who changes water to wine, one hundred fifty gallons of it. He is the one who changes me, who makes my heart glad.

A servant hands me a cup, and I laugh again. He grins at me, and we chuckle together. I raise the cup to my lips and taste this new wine, wine made from water when all we had relied on had run out.

The new wine is glorious. It fills me with wonder. It fills me with joy.

And I see. I have waited, and now I am changed.

I was water. I have become fine wine.

The Wine of Wonder

The fine art of waiting. I shake my head even as I type the words. *Waiting.* I smile a bit, because if there's anything I know something about, it's waiting. I'm an expert. Like Mary, I should practically have a PhD in the art.

Years of infertility taught me all about how to wait. And then, it taught me something else. It taught me that God is the God of joy. He is the one who transforms not only my circumstances but my very self.

My story, like Mary's, culminates at the moment of emptiness. Empty wine jugs. Empty water jars. Empty cups. Waiting hearts.

Ten years I'd traveled on the infertility journey with only a miscarriage to show for all our hopes and efforts. Ten long years of soaring hopes and crashing disappointments.

And now it was Mother's Day. The worst day of the whole year. I almost stayed home. I almost pleaded sickness. But I didn't.

Instead, I clutched my Bible to my chest, sat in the very back of the church, and ached as the mothers were called up front to be honored.

I sat there in my emptiness while my hopes dried up.

The moms sauntered back to their seats with pink carnations in their hands. I hunched my shoulders and squirmed lower in my seat. They smiled and laughed. I tried not to cry.

Then the music began. An old hymn, one that I'd heard before, but this time it was different.

My Jesus I love thee, I know thou art mine …

I didn't sing. I couldn't. Not today. There was no more wine.

My gracious Redeemer, my Savior art thou …

Gracious? Really? I'd wept, I'd worried, I'd come to him with my sorrow. And I was still empty.

The final line of the verse echoed to my soul. *If ever I loved thee, my Jesus 'tis now.*

Now? As I sat before him in my barrenness, as I watched the women with children honored? As I faced Mother's Day and had my heart broken all over again? Now?

Then, it was as if he whispered to me a single word: *Woman …*

And like Mary, I knew what he was asking. He wanted me to stop demanding he "fix it" and instead trust him even when things hadn't happened the way I hoped, the way I prayed and planned. In the face of emptiness, disappointment, and pain, he was asking me to love him anyway. He wanted me to let go of what I wanted from him and simply say, "Whatever you say, I will do."

I will trust.

I will love.

Even today.

Especially today.

When the wine casks were empty? When discouragement and pain and shame and despair were screaming through my soul? Let go and simply trust him? Follow him?

Yes.

It seemed impossible.

I let go anyway.

I didn't expect a miracle.

I got one anyway.

I sang. I sang with everything that was in me. I sang with tears flowing down my face and with a broken heart. And I was transformed. Because, if ever I loved him, it was now. Now, in the emptiness. Now, in the barrenness. Now, in the midst of a Mother's Day celebration that underscored everything that God had not done for me.

Now is when he asked me to declare my love for him.

And I was forever changed.

The very next morning, the nurse from the fertility clinic called. They had checked my blood work. I was pregnant. Nine months later, Bethany would be born.

He is the God of abundance. The God who takes emptiness and turns it into joy.

God turned my water into wine.

And all we could do was rejoice.

Because when we were all out of options, when all the casks and cups and jugs were empty, God did not just do a miracle, but he also gave us a sign. A sign of the type of Messiah, the type of God, he really is. He is the God of abundance. The God who transforms. The God who takes emptiness and turns it into joy.

Temptations

Like me, Mary waited a lot of years to see the angel's words fulfilled, to see the words of the Magnificat come into being. She'd pondered words and prophecies in her heart. She'd watched, she'd hoped, she'd raised a son of the Torah in the best way she knew how.

But at this point in the story, Jesus had come to manhood nearly two decades earlier. He'd been a carpenter in their hometown. And it seems that he'd cared for his family since Joseph's death (whenever that occurred). But he'd not made a big splash in Jerusalem. He'd not become a religious leader, nor a military one. Only recently had he begun to gain a few disciples: Andrew, Simon (whom he renamed Cephas/Peter), Philip, and Nathanael. And what a ragtag bunch they were!

Still, something was stirring. Something was starting. But it wasn't much. John testified that Jesus was the Lamb of God. Jesus was baptized in the Jordan. And Mary must have heard the rumors of the dove that descended there. But then Jesus spent forty days in the desert. He fasted all of those days and must have returned thin and emaciated.

What Mary didn't know is that at the end of those forty days, Jesus was tempted to do and be everything Mary was waiting for (see Matt. 4:1–11).

- He was tempted to perform his first miracle by changing stones into bread to satiate his own hunger. He was tempted to do his inaugural miracle to provide for his own needs. But Jesus resisted that temptation. Instead, his first miracle would be to transform water to wine for the benefit of others. It would be done quietly, almost secretively, and would not be called a miracle at all. It would be a sign, a sign of the kingdom he was initiating—a kingdom not about providing for our own needs but instead like a banquet where the wine of joy is in abundance and offered to all.

- He was tempted to throw himself off the temple in Jerusalem so that all in the great city could see the angels swooping down to rescue him. He was tempted to proclaim his messiahship in a grand and glorious way, to be honored by all. He resisted that temptation too. Instead, he would go to a wedding in the tiny, out-of-the-way village of Cana, a mere eight miles from Jesus' hometown of Nazareth, and he would bring joy to a relatively small group of people. And only his mother, some servants, and perhaps his disciples would know of it. The sign at the wedding in Cana would not be a path to his personal glory but, instead, a sign of joy.

- He was tempted to claim all the kingdoms and glory of the world by bowing down to Satan. He did not. Instead, he would choose the way of transformation—not to claim the glory of the world but to transform the world and the people in it to form a new kingdom, a kingdom symbolized by water turned to wine.

The Fruit of Waiting

But Mary didn't know all that. All she knew was that she'd been waiting a very long time.

And so came this event, a wedding, of all things—a time of joy, celebration, and happiness for the bride and groom and everyone who knew them. Commentator Andreas Kostenberger says, "Jewish weddings were important and joyful occasions in the lives of the bride and the groom and their extended families, and the entire community joined in the celebration."

But they ran out of wine. The old wine had dried up; it was gone. What was old, what they provided for themselves, wasn't enough. It had run out. And with it, all the joy, celebration, and happiness would dry up as well. Those things would be replaced by shame.

So Mary turned to her son. She stated the need: "They have no more wine" (v. 3). Jesus had done no miracles up to this point, so it was unlikely that Mary was looking for one here. But she was looking for something.

New Testament scholar Scot McKnight says, "Mary's observation that the wine was gone was filled with expectation that Jesus should fix the problem.... It is clear that Jesus understood his mother's words as carrying an honor code, fifth-commandment-claim-as-a-mother on him to do something about the wine."

Mary's expectation is what made Jesus' first word to her so powerful. He did not call her "Mother," or "Mom," or any endearment that would hint at their special relationship. Instead, he called her what he would call many other women who would follow him in his ministry. He called her *gunai*, meaning simply "woman." It was not a disrespectful, harsh, or rude name. In fact, this is what he would call the woman of Samaria (John 4:21), the woman caught in adultery (8:10), and Mary Magdalene (20:15), all women who would be his followers, his disciples. He would also use this word again of Mary when he was on the cross (19:26).

So while the word conveyed no disrespect, it also called for a new type of relationship between them. In the use of this one simple word, Jesus was calling Mary to be transformed. He was asking her to stop being "mother" and instead become a follower, a disciple. Subtly, gently, he was asking for her to let go of her special privileges as "mom" and instead submit to his timing, his will, which was ultimately God's timing, God's will.

Commentator Gary Burge says, "It is unusual for [Jesus] to address his mother this way when other titles would be preferred. In some sense, Mary is presuming on her relationship with him as her son (Luke 2:51), yet Jesus is redefining this: He cannot act under her authority but must instead follow the course that has been determined for him by God."

Next, Jesus said something that causes translators to struggle. The NIV says, "Why do you involve me?" The KJV says, "What have I to do with thee?" The NASB says, "What does that have to do with us?" The RSV says, "What have you to do with me?" The NLT says, "That's not our problem." You can see the difficulty when you look directly at the Greek, which literally says, "What to me and to you?" What? What's that supposed to mean? It's difficult to determine. But one thing seems clear in the Greek: Jesus was not saying, "Oh sure, let me whip up some wine at your command, Mom!" And by mentioning himself and Mary separately, he was emphasizing some kind of distinction between them. His question created a separation between his mother and himself.

Jesus then went on to address what may be the unspoken question behind Mary's statement. Maybe she was asking, "Is it time? Is it finally time? I've waited so long...."

And Jesus' answer to this was: "My hour has not yet come" (v. 4). Every time the word "hour" is used in the gospel of John, it means the time when Jesus will be glorified by being crucified (see John 7:30; 12:23; 13:1). It means the hour of his death on a cross. And Jesus was claiming to be the only one who knew when that hour would come. He knew the will of God, his Father, both at the present and into the future.

Transformation

Then something strange happened. Mary changed. She didn't insist, she didn't assert, she didn't again appeal to her special relationship with Jesus. She saw what Jesus was saying: that he couldn't be manipulated. In the wilderness, Satan could tempt Jesus, but he couldn't manipulate him. Mary couldn't either.

D. A. Carson says, "We must not avoid the conclusion that Jesus, by rebuking his mother, however courteously, declares, at the beginning of his ministry, his utter freedom from any kind of human advice, agenda, or manipulation. He has embarked on his ministry, the purpose of his coming; his only lodestar is his heavenly Father's will (5:30; 8:29)."

So Mary became a follower, a disciple. She was no longer the same woman who just came to Jesus as a mother and stated a need. Instead, she was a truster. She was submitted.

Mary became a follower, a disciple. She was submitted.

This change was evidenced in the way Mary turned to the servants and said, "Do whatever he tells you" (2:5). She simply trusted Jesus. In the waiting, she chose to trust that Jesus would do whatever was right, whatever was best.

And what Jesus did was transform. Just as he transformed Mary, he transformed water jugs used for the Jewish rites of purification into vessels of celebration. He transformed the water itself into new wine, better wine than anyone at the party had tasted before. And not just a little. Jesus gave between 120 to 150 gallons of this new wine, more than could be consumed by the partygoers. He gave in abundance.

"This is the message of Cana. Jesus has come to transform," says Burge. The symbolism of these transformations is hard to miss. First, in Jewish life, wine was the symbol of celebration, of joy. The joy and celebration that the wedding party provided for themselves was gone. It could no longer provide what was needed. Likewise, there is no more joy in providing for our own celebration. We need something new.

Something New

Jesus saw the empty jars for the Jewish rites of purification. He saw symbols of the old order, the old way to become pure. They were empty. They no longer worked or were effective for their purposes. What we have relied on in our old rites of religion are empty.

He told the servants, those whose job it was to bring the wine, to carry joy to others, to fill the jars with water. The servants couldn't provide wine. They could only obey. And they did. They didn't question, they didn't raise an eyebrow and say, "What? That's crazy; that won't help!" They remembered they were servants and did what they were told.

And the water was turned to wine. Abundantly. Joy came. And it was better than anything that had come before. After tasting the water-that-became-wine, the master of the feast said to the groom, "Everyone brings out the choice wine first and then the cheaper wine after the guests have had too much to drink; but you have saved the best till now" (v. 10). Jesus changes our water into choice wine, the best wine ... the best and fullest and most fragrant joy.

Which is why John calls what Jesus did a sign—not so much a miracle but a sign. Of what? Of the kingdom of God! In the Gospels, the kingdom is often likened to a wedding feast (see Matt. 22; 25; Rev. 19). Furthermore, since weddings were the primary celebrations that Jewish people enjoyed throughout the year, they also became the symbols of messianic celebration. "When Jews reflected on what heaven or the arrival of Messiah would be like ... the wedding banquet was the foremost model that came to mind," says Burge. In both Hosea 2:22 and Amos 9:13–14, for example, the abundance of wine in the land is linked to the Day of the Lord, to blessings and joy for the people. It is new life. It is abundance. It is God in the party.

That's the result of transformation. That's what comes of waiting. Jesus isn't at our beck and call. He isn't about doing what we tell him to do. He is in the business of transforming our water to wine, our empty jars into vessels of joy, our very selves into disciples and servants of a kingdom of celebration.

When we are weary of our old ways of finding happiness, when our reliance on ourselves and our own provisions have failed, when we're ready to trust God's timing and say, "Whatever he says," then, in his timing, he will take our plain water and make it into a thing of joy.

That is the fine art of waiting—to trust, to watch, to say, "Whatever he tells me, I will do."

So, as you wait, and wait, and wait, and it seems that God will never do anything, you have a choice. You can choose to push, assert, demand that life go the way you want it to go based on the relationship you think you have with Jesus. Or you can choose to follow. You can choose to trust. You can decide to do whatever he says, whether it seems to make sense to you or not.

That is the fine art of waiting—to trust, to watch, to say, "Whatever he tells me, I will do." And then, when the time is right, when the jars are empty, he will do his transforming work.

He might even do a miracle, a sign of what is to come…. And you will taste the exquisite flavor of his wondrous joy.

Who Is This God?

When I look back at my pregnancy with Bethany, I discover something odd. I find that our miracle baby wasn't the final answer to my infertility; rather, she was the confirmation of what I had learned through it. She showed me how I had been changed in the waiting. She showed me that only in transformation can there be found real joy.

I think it was that way for Mary too. When Jesus turned water into wine, it wasn't an answer to Mary's waiting. It wasn't the moment when all would become just as she'd always dreamed. Instead, it was a moment that reflected what had happened inside her. In the waiting, she, too, had been changed. Transformed. And the miracle itself wasn't the answer to prayer. Rather, it was a revealing of the type of Messiah Jesus would be, the type of God he always had been.

This is the God who took a childless man from Ur and transformed him into the father of the nation who would birth God-become-man. That is the story of Abraham, father of Israel.

This is the God who took a foreign woman from Moab, made her a widow, then transformed her into the ancestor of a king. That is the story of Ruth, who would be great-grandmother to King David.

This is the God who took a shepherd boy and made him a king after God's own heart. That is the story of David, the king who received the promise of a royal line that would never end.

This is the God who took a lowly shepherd of Tekoa and transformed him into a prophet of God. That is the story of Amos, whose prophecies would stand the test of time to be read even today.

This is the God who took a virgin from the backwoods of Galilee and made her into the most blessed woman in all of history. That is Mary's story.

This is my God, who took an infertile woman and made her the mother of six ... who transformed her on the journey. That is my story.

After all, I never planned on infertility. I expected to get married and have kids, no problem, just like everyone else I knew. But

God's plan was to lead me down a different road to show me truths about himself that I never would have seen otherwise. Through the longing for a baby, I learned that I must yearn more for God. Through month after month of trying and failing, I learned that I'm not the god of my life; he is. There are things I cannot control, cannot achieve, no matter how hard I try. Through prayers that went unanswered, I learned I couldn't measure God's love for me based on my circumstances.

But most of all, God showed me how to pry my white-knuckled fingers off my own hopes and dreams for my life in order to embrace *his* dreams, *his* vision for who I am. He taught me to live the life he has given me with love and hope even when it's not the life I dreamed. He taught me to choose to love anyway, to believe anyway, to trust anyway. He transformed me.

So, when the wine has run out, when there seems to be no more hope ...

He is the God who transforms water into wine.

He is the God of transformation.

He is the God of joy.

CHAPTER 10

God, Have You Lost Your Mind?
Jesus' Family Takes Charge

MARK 3:20 – 21, 31 – 35

᭙

God, have you lost your senses? I've muttered those words. Mary has too. We know, because the gospel of Mark tells us, "When his family heard ... they went to take charge of him, for they said, 'He is out of his mind'" (Mark 3:21).

God, are you crazy? There are those times when life doesn't make sense, when all our expectations are shattered, and we wonder, we doubt, we question, we wrestle with this God who refuses to conform to who we want him to be.

> *It seems that God himself has lost his mind, because the truth you believe does not result in the life you expect.*

God, are you really out of your mind? We think so when we've prayed and prayed and the opposite thing happens, when we've trusted and obeyed and things just get worse.

I've been there. Mary's been there. Maybe you have too.

Have you walked that shadowed valley where truth is tainted with unmet expectations, where doubts are colored by old paradigms not yet broken, not yet remade? Perhaps you've read the promises and believed them. You've had faith, you've waited, you've trusted. And yet ...

It seems that God himself has lost his mind, because the truth you believe does not result in the life you expect.

Who is this God?

And what do we do when he isn't the God we've expected him to be?

Mary faced that question. I imagine it happened something like this:

Mary Tells Her Story

My boy is out of his mind. It's the only explanation for what he's done, hasn't done. I thought after Cana, after the water-turned-to-wine, things would be different. I thought being his disciple would be—well, would not be like this. I was changed, but oh, now I just don't understand.

I know what a messiah is supposed to look like, act like. I know, because I sang of it. I've read the Scriptures, I've pondered in my heart.

And I know that this Messiah is not like I expected.

Lord, is this what I waited for?

He's out of his mind.

He's chosen his disciples. Rabble, all of them. Fishermen, tax collectors, a zealot. Not a respectable one in the bunch. And he's gone about healing and preaching. He's not studying the law or teaching in the temple. He's wandering the countryside with a crowd of vagabonds.

They say he even healed a man's shriveled hand on the Sabbath. On the Sabbath! Oh, didn't he know, didn't he realize?

Lord, has our son gone crazy?

I've heard rumors. The Pharisees have met with the Herodians. They plan to destroy him. Did we run to Egypt for nothing? Will those of Herod kill him in the end?

God of Israel, I gave my life for this boy, for your Anointed One. Will he now treat his life so callously? Will he fall so far below all I've sung about, all I've hoped for, expected?

The scribes and Pharisees, the respected religious leaders of my people, think he's possessed by Beelzebub. They think he's of the devil.

I just think he's crazy.

And now it's the last straw. I've heard that he has such a throng of riffraff around him—prostitutes, slaves, loathsome tax collectors—that he and his disciples cannot even eat.

One thing a mother knows: her son has to eat.

I need to bring him home. Feed him fresh-baked bread dipped in olive oil, cook a young goat for him and his friends, let him turn water into wine again.

I pause. He did do that, didn't he? I remember it so well. One moment an insurmountable problem, the next, six great jars filled with choice wine.

After that, I thought ... I expected ...

He's supposed to be the Messiah, after all. He's supposed to set our people free. He's supposed to conquer Rome so Israel will rise again under him, our Davidic Messiah-King.

This itinerant rabbi looks nothing like he should.

And now it's my job to fix it, set him back on his proper course, help him to become the Son of God he is supposed to be.

I gather my shawl around me. Then I gather his brothers. We will go. We will find him. We will bring him home. And then he will behave as I think he ought. He will be who I want him to be.

So we go. We walk. I run. Just a little. Because that's what I do with this boy. I run to save him.

He is not difficult to find. We see the large crowd spilling out the doorway of a house on the main road. Men are standing on tiptoes trying to see inside. Children peek under their legs. Even women have come to hear him.

We come to the opening. The crowd does not part.

"Excuse me, we've come to see Jesus."

A few look back at me. "Haven't we all?" someone mumbles.

"Let us through," James commands.

But no one moves.

Simon tries. But there's no hope. We cannot get through to see him, to seize him, to take him home until he comes to his senses.

"We must see Jesus! I am his mother. These are his brothers!" That should shock them. That should get them to move aside and let us in.

But still they don't move.

"His mother? His brothers?" someone says.

"Yes."

"I'll tell him."

Now I am the one standing on tiptoes. Still I cannot see Jesus. But I do see a man sidling through the crowd. Then the man speaks. "Your mother and brothers are outside looking for you."

I smile. Now Jesus will come. He knows I am here, waiting ... expecting.

But the crowd doesn't part, and I do not see him coming toward me. I do not see him at all.

Then I hear him. I hear him saying an impossible thing. I cannot believe I'm hearing it. I cannot believe he's saying it:

Who are my mother and my brothers?
Here are my mother and my brothers!

He's speaking of them, the ones around him! He is not speaking of me. I'm on the outside, an outsider. How could this be? Who am I? Who is his mother if not me?

Whoever does God's will is my brother and sister and mother!

I crumble to the ground, his words like swords in my soul. I don't understand. Who is this man? Who is this son? Who is this out-of-his-mind Messiah?

And will I choose to be his family if he refuses to be who I want him to be? Will I still be his mother if he breaks my every expectation, shatters my every vision, defies my carefully constructed image of who he is meant to be?

He is his Father's Son.

Oh, Lord, maybe I'm the one who's losing my mind.

God beyond Expectation

We're not much different from Mary. Life doesn't turn out as we expect. God doesn't turn out as we expect. So we think he's crazy. Maybe the Messiah has lost his mind. We need to set him straight. We need to explain to him the type of God he's supposed to be.

Sounds silly when we say it that way.

But when our expectations are broken, we often look at God as if something's wrong with *him*. We lose faith because he hasn't lived up to *our* expectations, he hasn't conformed to *our* image of him, he hasn't acted according to *our* ideas of what's right and good.

So what do we do when life as we experience it clashes with our expectation of what life should look like, how God should act on our behalf? We glimpse God's dream for us, we surrender our own dreams, and then our expectations paint a glorious picture of everything wondrous that life will be.

But it isn't.

Wait a minute! We believed. We surrendered. We know what is true. Yet life looks nothing like we thought it would. And God looks nothing like we thought he would!

What then? What do we do when experience and expectation conflict?

So what do we do when life as we experience it clashes with our expectation of what life should look like?

Expecting Easy

For me it's been an ongoing battle, one that God brought to mind again recently when my seven-year-old twins were baptized. The water sparkled as brightly as their eyes as they crossed their arms, plugged their noses, and prepared for the moment of submersion. Each was a little scared, a little nervous, but eager to commit her whole life, surrender her whole self, to her Savior. It was a beautiful moment, a beautiful decision, and their faces glowed with the wonder of it.

Afterward, one of our pastors leaned over and looked into little Bria's eyes. "Do you think it will be easier to follow Jesus now?"

A grin split her face. "Oh yes!" She said the words with such enthusiasm, her voice alight with the wonder, the hope, the expectation of a songs-and-daisies walk with her Lord.

It broke my heart.

Because, yes, it is easier to follow Jesus when you're fully committed to him. It's easier to grasp the hope and wonder when you've obeyed, when your heart is his. It's easier. And yet it's not.

Because I know enough of the road ahead to see that Bria's life with God won't be all songs and daisies. Even though I'm sure that Jesus loves her deeply, that he died and rose again so that she might live with him, I know that life won't look anything like she expects. It won't even look anything like what I expect for her.

It will be filled with some glorious moments, some moments when Jesus is so clear, so vibrant that Bria's faith will soar. But it will also be filled with other moments, moments of confusion and heartache, when Jesus looks nothing like she expected him to be.

There will be times when Bria weeps and wonders why God hasn't intervened like she believed he would. There will be days of intense doubt, heartbreaking disappointment, broken despair. There will be seasons when her walk with God is anything but easy.

Because if there's one thing I've learned, it's that God explodes expectations. He does not conform to our view, but instead he conforms us to his.

Skipping Three

I should know this. I've learned it often enough but maybe never more than when God gave me the twins to begin with. Back when my husband and I were engaged, we talked about children. We dreamed. We chose names. We decided how many we'd like to have. Three children. We'd always expected three.

Instead, we wondered if we'd have any. But then, eleven years after marriage, we had Bethany at last. With her we drew a little closer to our plans. We tried again ... and miscarried. We tried some more. More IUI's (intrauterine inseminations), all failing. Two difficult IVF cycles. Failed. And then, after two years of intensive treatments, we were finally pregnant again. Joelle was born in May.

By the following summer, we were ready to try again, ready for that baby number three we had always hoped for, had once expected.

Baby number three ... and then all would be right in our world.

So we went back to the doctor again for a frozen embryo transfer. Embryos are frozen in pairs. The odds are small they will both survive the "thaw" (basically, rehydration) and continue to develop. The odds are smaller (less than 1 percent) that they'll both grow into babies. And then add in the tiny odds that they'll both be healthy and survive to term. Itty-bitty odds.

Our God is the God of itty-bitty odds.

Both of our thawed embryos survived the initial transfer. Both grew in the womb. And on a sunny Tuesday in July, both were born as healthy baby girls, one blonde-haired beauty and one beautiful brunette. Against all odds, we had twin girls. And in their birth, I saw the hand of my crazy God.

Because everything survived … except my expectations.

Those had to be left at the door.

Because I could do the math: one child, two children … four children. Only one number was missing — the one I had chosen. The one I was aiming for. I'd planned for three. I'd expected three. And three would be the one number we wouldn't have, the number we would skip.

He is the God who calls us to leave our expectations at the door and come in to sit at his feet.

In their birth, God was showing me that he is indeed a crazy God. He is the God who breaks all expectations, who shatters preconceptions, who wants nothing more than to blow apart my ideas of who he is and replace them with a true vision of who he *really* is.

He is the God who calls us to leave our expectations at the door and come in to sit at his feet.

I had to learn to accept that God. Mary did too.

The Expected Messiah

Mary's expectations weren't bad ones. After all, she had learned what to expect from reading her Bible!

This is what they expected:

- a leader like Moses (see Deut. 18:15 – 18)
- a prophet who was even greater than Elijah or Jeremiah (see Matt. 16:13 – 16)

- a Davidic king (see 2 Sam. 7)
- a ruler who would combine the glory of David with the wisdom of Solomon (see 1 Kings 3 and Isa. 11)

As Scot McKnight says, "The future Messiah would be like Moses, mentoring everyone to obey the Torah; like a prophet, declaring the word of the Lord in thunderous and poetic terms; like David the king, sitting on the throne in peace after conquering the land and routing the enemies of Israel; and like Solomon, offering wisdom to the people."

But this wandering rabbi with his ragtag bunch of followers didn't look like that at all. Instead of being a forceful leader and an amazing prophet, Jesus was a man whom the religious leaders scorned and only the crowds crowded. Sometimes, he couldn't even get a decent meal (see Matthew 12:1; Mark 2:23; Luke 6:1). He taught out in the countryside, in boats, in houses. He was no king in Jerusalem, gathering the powerful under his authority to conquer Rome. "[Mary's] … problem was Jesus himself: He didn't act like the Messiah she (and everyone else) expected," says McKnight.

He was a homeless teacher.

He was a healer not of the powerful but of the poor.

To the crowds, he was a sideshow. An anomaly. A curiosity.

To the religious leaders, he was a threat.

To his followers, he was more. But even they did not understand him.

To his family, he was a man out of his mind, a man who held the promises of God and wasn't living up to them. He was a son, a brother, who needed to be told how to be whom God wanted him to be. And they were going to do just that.

We see Mary's broken expectations most clearly when we look back at them in the Magnificat. She sang of the promised Messiah. She sang of her son. And everything she sang was true, but oh, how Jesus would stretch, shatter, and remold her expectations in order to fulfill them in a new way, in a new era. By reexamining the Magnificat, we see why she thought Jesus had lost his mind.

Expectations from the Magnificat

Let's revisit Mary's hopes, dreams, and, yes, expectations from the Magnificat. She sang:

> *He has scattered those who are proud*
> *in their inmost thoughts.*
> *He has brought down rulers from their thrones*
> *but has lifted up the humble. (Luke 1:51–52)*

In these verses, "Mary places herself squarely in solidarity with all God's people and recognizes in her own experience the establishing, at least in principle, of all that the faith of God's people had encouraged them someday to expect from God," claims John Nolland. And they expected much. Using images harkening back to the defeat of Pharaoh and the rescue of God's people from their slavery in Egypt, Mary believed God would again deliver the humble and defeat the proud. He would fulfill the covenant at last.

But would he? Yes and no. At the time Mary uttered her words, the Roman Empire had conquered Israel and ruled it for decades. Herod the Great had lorded over the poor for around thirty-five of those years. So it makes sense that Mary would be clinging to the hope of a king in David's line to take the place of Herod. That's what all the Jews would have been hoping for and expecting from a messiah.

But Mary was not witnessing the Roman Empire taken down. And she wouldn't in her lifetime. She wouldn't even see the arrogant Herodian rulers defeated. Rather, her son, the Messiah, the Redeemer who was to free Israel, would be condemned by a Roman representative and executed by Rome. And the son of Herod the Great, Herod Antipas, would have a part in the arrest and death of her son. She would not see her people lifted up. Instead, Jesus himself would be lifted up on a Roman cross. And her people? In AD 70 the great city of Jerusalem would be destroyed by the Roman army led by Titus, who would become the emperor of Rome. All of this would defy every expectation and yet fulfill every prophecy and promise.

The reason? Because God's mercy isn't married to might but to weakness—to the frailty of a human body dying on a Roman cross. His mercy, his might, would be in carrying the sins of all the world and dying for them, for Mary, for Israel, for all of us. His mighty deed would not be conquering Rome but conquering death itself. God's Son would bring Satan down from his throne and defeat death. Victory over sin, Satan, and death—that is mercy; that is might, exemplified in a way that Mary never could have dreamed—larger, grander, more wondrous than even she could imagine. But it would take the shattering of her expectations to accomplish it. It would take sorrow, loss, defeat, and death to truly bring about the promises that filled her song. And this moment, when she stood outside the door, calling for Jesus to come out and be who she wanted him to be, was the beginning of all that would come. It was the beginning of the rumblings against him, the complaints that would soon lead him directly to the cross.

It would take sorrow, loss, defeat, and death to truly bring about the promises that filled Mary's song.

Jesus wasn't, and wouldn't be, the military leader Mary expected. He would be more.

Mary's song continued ...

> *He has filled the hungry with good things*
> *but has sent the rich away empty. (Luke 1:53)*

Would the rich suddenly be overthrown in a grand revolution? No. Would manna rain down from heaven as it had in the desert after the people of Israel escaped from Egypt? Not exactly. This Jesus wasn't doing what was needed in order to rise to an earthly throne and lavish gifts on the poor from his kingly seat in Jerusalem. But Jesus would send away the rich young ruler (see Luke

18:18–30) and feed five thousand men and feed another four thousand later (see Matt. 14:13–21 and 15:29–38). He would fill the hungry and send away the rich. But he would do more. He would fill those hungering for righteousness (see Matt. 5:6) not with wafer-like manna but with himself. He himself would be the manna from heaven. He would be the Bread of Life (see John 6:35).

When Mary sang, she never would have expected that.

> *He has helped his servant Israel,*
> *remembering to be merciful*
> *to Abraham and his descendants forever*
> *just as he promised our ancestors. (Luke 1:54–55)*

While writing this and pondering Mary's words and reflecting on her hopes, I paused to check my email. A message came in from friend and fellow writer Jim Denney. It said:

> Hamas rockets are falling on Jerusalem. Possible intent is to provoke Israel into a ground invasion of Hamas-controlled territory in Gaza, and draw in Egypt. The Egyptian government, now under heavy Muslim Brotherhood influence, blames Israel for the violence. Egypt could easily be drawn in, and is only restrained by the cash flow from the Camp David accords. Hezbollah is making sword-rattling noise in Lebanon. Syria is in chaos, and a clash with Israel would strengthen Bashar al Assad against his internal enemies. And Iran calls for the extermination of Israel on a near-weekly basis. Israel is in an extremely dangerous situation right now, ringed by hostility and under attack.

Mary would have wept to hear of it, wept to know that the coming of the Messiah didn't mean peace and prosperity for a physical nation of Israel even two thousand years later. Not political peace. And not for Abraham's physical descendants.

Mary would see no political revolution, but she would see the whole world turned upside down. She would see expectations broken so promises could come true. She would see death itself turned into life. She would see what would seem impossible, and it would look nothing like she ever could have expected.

Jesus was not out of his mind. No, he was shattering Mary's old paradigms in order to rebuild them. It wouldn't be the last time Jesus shattered expectations. Later, outside the temple in Jerusalem he would say, "Destroy this temple, and I will raise it again in three days" (John 2:19). The Jews who heard him could think only of the temple building, but Jesus was speaking about the temple of his body, the true place where God himself dwelled. The understanding and expectations of the Jews were limited, temporal, and physical, just like Mary's. And just like Jesus fulfilled his promise about the temple in a way no one expected through his death and resurrection, so too would he fulfill the expectations that Mary expressed in the Magnificat. He would fulfill every word and yet do it in ways no one would expect, not even Mary.

Breaking Expectations

That's what Jesus is about—breaking Mary's expectations and breaking ours. He does it to rebuild us, to free us, to call us deeper into God's will. We see it in the words he spoke when he heard that his mother and brothers were outside calling for him.

> *"Who are my mother and my brothers?" he asked.*
> *Then he looked at those seated in a circle around him and said,*
> *"Here are my mother and my brothers! Whoever does God's will is*
> *my brother and sister and mother." (Mark 3:33–35)*

Ouch! That must have hurt. But Jesus wasn't rejecting his mother and family. Instead, he was inviting them in. He was saying, "Come, be my mother, be my brothers ... by sitting in this circle around me." He would not come out to be who they wanted him to be. Instead, he was asking them to accept who he is and follow him, in the very moment when their expectations of him were most broken, at exactly the time he was refusing to be the Messiah they wanted.

Just when the image of Messiah in the Magnificat clashed most with the image of the wandering rabbi before her, Jesus asked Mary to trust. Trust that he is Messiah. Trust that he knows what he's doing. Trust and come into the circle.

Jesus is about breaking Mary's expectations and breaking ours. He does it to rebuild us, to free us, to call us deeper into God's will.

He says the same to us. We all come to this place of broken expectations where we are at the door, calling for Jesus to come out and be who we want him to be.

At those life moments, to get on the "inside" near Christ, we must focus on doing his will, doing what we know is right, even when life doesn't make sense. Even when God doesn't make sense. We can stay outside the door, calling for him to come out so we can take charge of him, calling for him to come out and be the type of God we want him to be. Or we can go in, sit at his feet, and leave our expectations at the door.

That was Mary's choice, and it's ours as well. We, too, have to decide.

What Will You Choose?

As he did for Mary, Jesus breaks in to shatter our old paradigms, to remake us. And life doesn't turn out the way we expect. God doesn't act like we expect. The promises don't seem to be coming true. Our life looks like a crazy mess. We lose our job; we can't pay our bills; a child rebels; a loved one dies; cancer hits; we face divorce, infertility, failure in ministry. Bombs fall into our lives and break us apart. We face the loss of what we expected life to look like if we follow Christ, surrender to him.

So we wonder ...

Am I doing something wrong?
Has God forgotten me?
Has he betrayed me?

Are the promises just not true?

God, have you lost your mind?

We wonder, we doubt, we worry. We question God's goodness, we call to him from the outside. And all the time it is not us or God or the promises that have failed, it's our expectations that have betrayed us. They have taken the truth and whispered lies in our ears. We operate in the paradigm we know—the world's paradigm. We see the promises through the lens of what the world says is blessed—success, victory, being well fed and well loved. The problem is that true success, true victory, being truly well fed and well loved look little like we're taught to believe. Sometimes success looks like failure; sometimes it looks like we've been abandoned; sometimes it looks like death itself.

> *We follow an out-of-the-box Messiah. We forget that every promise will be fulfilled ... but in ways we never dreamed.*

We've forgotten that we serve an unexpected Christ, we follow an out-of-the-box Messiah. We forget that every promise will be fulfilled ... but in ways we never dreamed. Mary would learn this. Every single line she sang in the Magnificat would come true, but not a single line in the way she must have expected. And in the journey, she would become who God always intended her to be. She would become mother of the Messiah by a means she never would have wanted, never would have dreamed. She would see victory beyond imagination. And she would see it when all seemed lost.

So, the question is, when life takes a turn, when things are nothing as expected, will you still believe, will you still sing? Will you still say, "My soul magnifies the Lord?" This is the Christ that comes into our lives, the one who fulfills every promise and defies every expectation. The one who showers his mercy, who lifts us up in our pain, who fills us in ways we cannot foresee. The one who remakes us … beyond our expectations, beyond anything we ever could have dared to dream.

Like Mary, we, too, must choose. When God seems to have lost his mind, will you still walk through the door, sit at his feet, and do the will of the Father? Or will you keep calling to him from outside the door? Will you cling to your picture of who God is supposed to be and insist he conform to your will instead of you to his?

Or will you trust that he is truly your Messiah when he doesn't behave the way you want? When life is nothing like you expect and prayers aren't answered the way you'd hoped, when God hasn't intervened, when the songs seem like delusional dreams, will you still trust him?

Will you go in and sit at the feet of the Savior?

Who Is This God?

Do we want an unexpected Messiah? Can we accept an out-of-the-box God? If God loves us, if he has a wonderful plan for our lives, doesn't that mean life should go well?

If God is sending the Messiah, if he is fulfilling his promises, doesn't that mean that Israel will be free?

Not exactly …

Because he is not who we expect him to be. He is not who Mary expected him to be. He is more. This God is both the promise maker and the expectation breaker.

The Promise Maker and the Expectation Breaker

Just as they were for Mary, broken expectations are an opportunity for God to remake our lives, to show us who he is in new and deeper ways. Our broken expectations are an opportunity for us to become his true family—the ones who do the will of God even when God doesn't do what we expect.

Jesus says, "And no one pours new wine into old wineskins.

Otherwise, the new wine will burst the skins; the wine will run out and the wineskins will be ruined" (Luke 5:37). We need new wineskins, a new and deeper understanding of who the Messiah really is.

So the answer is not to expect nothing, to have no "wineskins" at all, but rather to watch for the places in our lives where our expectations of how life should go, how God should act, become broken. These are the places where God is doing something new, showing us something deeper about himself. These are the places in our lives where he wants to free us from our worldly paradigms and give us a new vision, a new hope, based on the wonder of who he really is.

Don't take the easy way. Don't say, "Well, I just won't expect God to do anything." That's not what Mary did! Instead, she came to Jesus. She called for him. She listened. And she didn't get what she wanted. But she did get a clearer view of the truth of what kind of Messiah Jesus would be. And in it, she got a glimpse of the Father. And then she wrestled as God remade her, as God broke her expectations and yet fulfilled his promises. He will do the same for you.

God will fulfill his promises but in ways you never expect … and that is how he will draw you deeper, show you himself! We are broken, we are remade, by wrestling with the wonder of expectations shattered while promises are fulfilled. Wrestle and sing. Weep and wonder.

And ask: "Will I still walk this journey, knowing that the fulfillment of my song may not look anything like I expect? Will I still believe?"

When life goes awry and the songs seem like foolishness, will you come and sit in the inner circle? Will you do God's will, even when it leads to the foot of the cross?

CHAPTER 11

When Nightmares Come True

Jesus' Arrest, Beating, and Sentence

MATTHEW 26:47 – 27:44; MARK 14:43 – 15:32;
LUKE 22:47 – 23:43; JOHN 18:1 – 19:25

〰️

We heard the song as little children, sang it, and maybe even believed it:

> *When you wish upon a star*
> *Makes no difference who you are*
> *Anything your heart desires*
> *Will come to you ...*

Except it doesn't.

Yet still we wish, dream, and believe that God's favor means we will live our happily ever after today. Because if God really loves us, won't all our dreams come true?

Except they don't.

Prince Charming turns out less than charming. Our castle is foreclosed on. And sometimes the dragons get their way.

Sometimes the worst thing imaginable happens.

Where is God then? What does his favor, his love, mean then? Who is this God in the face of cancer, divorce, job loss, miscarriage?

Who is he when we find drugs in a child's bedroom, when the police show up at the door, when life falls apart and everything we were afraid would happen does?

Where is God when nightmares come true and everything we feared must be faced? Who do we believe in, rely on?

Mary believed, she hoped, she sang, she pondered ... and then she faced her worst nightmare-come-true: the arrest, beating, sentencing, and crucifixion of her Messiah-son.

Where is God, who is God, when nightmares come true and everything we feared must be faced? What do we believe then? Who do we believe in, rely on?

Mary had to face those questions.

For her it must have been something like this:

Mary Tells Her Story

My deepest fear. My darkest doubt. My nightmare.

Come true.

My son, the Messiah, the Savior of Israel, has been arrested, beaten, condemned.

I am here in Jerusalem for the Passover feast, just as I've always come since Jesus was a babe. Joseph used to bring us, and I remember a trip when Jesus was twelve. I didn't understand him then. I don't understand now.

How could he be arrested? Couldn't he stop it? Doesn't he know he could die?

The Messiah can't die.

A young man came to me in the night, disheveled and out of breath. Told me they had arrested my son. Men came — soldiers, crowds — but not only them; the priests came too.

The leaders of my people. Even Malchus, the high priest's own personal servant. They came by night to a garden with clubs and torches and swords. And they took him.

No one stopped them. Not his disciples, not the crowds who once loved him. Not even God.

God? Are you not his Father? Why didn't you protect him? Protect me.

And so I run. Just like I've done so many times. I ran to Egypt to save him from Herod. But a Herod has caught up to him now. I ran to Jerusalem to find him when he was twelve.

I run to find him now. But this time I am too late. Again he is surrounded by a crowd. Again the priests and teachers of the law are with him. But this time he is not okay. He is not safe. He is asking no questions. He is speaking no Scripture.

This is not his Father's house. It is *Gabbatha*, the Stone Pavement. The place of judgment.

I skid to a stop and stand here shaking in a courtyard with a crowd. The noonday sun beats down on us, illuminating the stones, the people, the priests, and my son, wavering on the platform before me. The governor from Rome, Pilate, sits in the judgment seat beside him. I look at the governor, his flowing robe, his clean-shaven face.

For a moment, I cannot look at my son. Then I dare. A glance steals my breath, constricts my heart. I barely recognize him. His eye is swollen, his clothes bloody. He looks like a lamb already slaughtered.

He is wearing a purple robe, as if to mock him. And on his head ... *Oh, Lord* ...

My soul shatters.

On his head is a crown made of the thorns of the *akanthos* bush. Blood runs down his forehead, his cheeks.

Akanthos, a symbol of my people's shame ...

How could they do this to the Messiah?

And yet isn't this exactly what I was afraid might happen? Isn't this why we came to take charge of him? The anger of the Pharisees, the fickleness of the crowd. I saw it all coming. Why didn't he?

Or did he?

I shiver and close my eyes. And I remember a man who would not come out. Would not be the son, the Messiah, I wanted him to be.

I couldn't rescue him then.

I can't rescue him now.

And somehow I know, as I stand behind this crowd, that he is not coming out to me now either. He will never come out again.

I hear his words from that moment ringing in my ears: "Whoever does the will of my Father ..."

And I know he will still not be the Messiah I want.

He will do the will of his Father.

But, Lord, how can this be your will?

Surely the Messiah will not die! Not my son, not yours.

Oh, God, rescue him ...

Just days ago the crowds welcomed him like David coming into his kingdom. They spread palm branches on the road, they cried, "Hosanna!" They sang, "Blessed is he who comes in the name of the Lord! Blessed is the king of Israel!" They threw down their coats so the colt's hooves would not even touch the dirt.

And I believed he rode in to claim his kingdom at last.

But this is no kingdom like I have ever imagined.

A king isn't beaten.

A king isn't bloody.

A king doesn't die a criminal's death.

But perhaps I should have known the moment they declared him blessed . . .

Pilate holds up his hand. "Behold your king!" he shouts.

I cover my face, peek through my fingers.

"Do you want me to release for you the king of the Jews?"

For a moment, hope soars through me.

And is crushed by a single word: "Barabbas!" The chief priests hiss the name.

"Release for us Barabbas!" the crowd shrieks. Barabbas, the murderer, the sinner. How could they call for Barabbas? Will the sinner not die for his crime? Will my son be killed in his stead?

It's not fair. It's not right.

I shiver as the manacles drop from Barabbas's wrists, as he steps forward, as a smile splits his face with shocking radiance.

Barabbas is free. My son is condemned.

And I hear a whisper through my soul: *You are all Barabbas* . . . Oh, God . . .

Pilate speaks again. "What shall I do with this Jesus?"

The question drives into me, becomes my own. "What shall I do with this Jesus?" *What shall I do with a Messiah destined to die?*

The crowd shouts again. "Away with him, away with him!" *No.*

They scream a word that pierces my very soul: "Crucify!"

"Shall I crucify your king?"

And the chief priests, the very leaders who are meant to show us how to follow our God, call out words I never thought they'd cry. "We have no king but Caesar!"

And so they have rejected their Messiah and claimed Caesar as king. The end has come for us all.

> The crowd shouts, louder, louder, until it becomes a chant. "Crucify him! Crucify him!"
>
> I crumble, on the ground, in the crowd, broken, while my son is led away to die.

Wonder in the Nightmare

I tremble as I think about what it must have been like for Mary to stand in that crowd and listen to her son being condemned to the most painful, horrific execution known to mankind. The Gospels don't say she was at his trial, but they do tell us she was at the foot of the cross. So I think it is reasonable to believe that she was here, too, hearing the crowds turn on Jesus, seeing them reject their Messiah, watching them turn her son over to the Gentiles for a criminal's death.

It was a mother's worst nightmare, made worse by all the promises of an angel, all the hopes of a mother's song, all the prophecies from a God she still believed.

The one thing she most feared had happened.

What would she do, what do we do, with nightmares-come-true?

That's a question I was forced to face a few years ago.

My Nightmare-Come-True

As we started a new round of infertility treatments, I asked God for one thing. One simple thing: no more miscarriages. I could face failure, but I didn't want to face miscarriage again, not after going through it twice before. Those had been the most awful experiences of my life. The soaring hope, the niggling fear, the crushing disappointment. The grief.

Anything but that.

So I prayed. And prayed. And started treatment.

Against the odds, the first cycle worked. A positive pregnancy test. A heartbeat at six weeks.

I rejoiced, thanked God, and started planning the nursery. I told the girls, and every night they prayed for their new baby. They wanted a brother. They prayed for a brother. Bethany, her seven-year-old heart just opening to the wonder of God's love; Joelle, four years old, her hands clasped, her eyes squeezed tight as she prayed for a "new bruver"; and the twins, toddlers still, barely learning what it meant to pray but knowing something important was happening.

Surely God would give them a brother. Surely God wouldn't let this baby die.

But he did.

At nine weeks, an ultrasound showed no heartbeat. No baby. Miscarriage. Again.

I drove home in a daze, then picked up Bethany and Joelle from school with tears in my eyes. Telling them was one of the worst moments of my life. "I'm sorry," I choked. "Baby died."

They cried. I cried. We wept and sobbed. And waited for another cycle.

The time came to try again. So I prayed and prayed and prayed.

The cycle worked. A positive pregnancy test. A heartbeat at six weeks. Less hope, more fear. More prayer. And apprehension.

I didn't tell the girls.

Then came the nine-week ultrasound that showed miscarriage again.

So I wept again. Waited. Again. Prayed. Again. Tried. Again.

Got pregnant again.

Had a miscarriage. Again.

And again.

One full year of trying, getting pregnant, and losing our precious babies four times in a row.

One thing I'd asked. One thing was denied. One simple thing.

Denied in quadruplicate. What was God doing? And where was his mercy?

I was broken, afraid, wrestling with a grief I didn't know what to do with, didn't know how to subdue.

Bad Dreams in the Night

Then, one night as I lay in bed, a scream echoed from the upstairs bedroom. I jolted upright.

Feet pattered down the stairs. The door flew open. A small body flung toward me.

"Bethany? Is that you?"

She nestled in my arms.

"What's wrong?"

She sniffed and tilted up her head. "I—I had a bad dream. There was a monster, and ... and ... and he was ..."

"Shhh." I rubbed my hand over her hair. "It's all right. You know what we do when we have a nightmare."

She pushed away from me. "But I did pray. I prayed and prayed and prayed. I asked God not to let me have any nightmares. But I had one anyway." She shuddered. "How come I still have bad dreams when I asked God to take them away?"

I gulped as she looked at me with her round, dark eyes. "Well, uh ..."

She stood silent, waiting.

And then I knew. I just knew what I had to say. I gathered her close. "Listen, sweetie, sometimes we pray and God doesn't answer the way we want him to."

Sometimes he does something crazy, sometimes he stays silent, sometimes he is condemned to die.

Sometimes the nightmares are real ...

She sniffled. "Then why pray?"

Why pray? Why trust? Why believe in a God who allows four miscarriages in a row? Who allows his own Son to die in a murderer's stead? Why?

I closed my lips. Words wouldn't come.

My husband rolled toward me in the bed. He reached out and touched Bethany's hair. "Because God wants us to learn to trust him when we're afraid and when nothing makes sense. If he took away all our nightmares, how would we ever learn to turn to him when we're scared?"

The words settled deep in my soul. Bryan meant them for Bethany. God meant them for me.

I tucked Bryan's answer deep into my heart and gave Bethany a kiss. "Go back to bed and think about how much God loves you. Then pray that he'll help you not be afraid but to trust him instead. Okay?"

> "God wants us to learn to trust him when we're afraid and when nothing makes sense."

She scooted off my lap. "All right."

I gave her a quick hug and sent her back to bed. Then I unfolded Bryan's words and looked at them long and hard.

Trust God? That's what he had said. Even when nightmares came true? When prayers went unanswered? When pain came—in quadruplicate?

I closed my eyes. Bryan's answer to Bethany was really God's answer to me. He was after more in my life, too, than just taking away my nightmares. I was on Mary's journey. And the God who called me was asking me to live a nightmare, face the death of the one(s) I loved, and still follow him. Follow him all the way to the cross ...

Mary Faced Her Fears

That's what Mary had to do.

I think the gospel writers intended us to see the correlation between what Jesus' mother and brothers intended to do in Mark 3:21 when they came to "take charge of him" and what happened in the Garden of Gethsemane when Jesus was arrested. Four times Matthew used the verb *krateo* (Matt. 26:48, 50, 55, 57) to talk about what the large crowd armed with swords and clubs did to Jesus. This single Greek word is translated a variety of ways in our English translations: "seize," "arrest," "capture." But in the Greek, it is the same word throughout Matthew 26 and also Mark 3. It means "to lay hands on someone in order to get him into one's power."

Mary and Jesus' brothers came to seize him, arrest him, take hold of him, take charge. They failed to do so. And now others had come, an armed and hostile crowd, to do the same. They succeeded.

The point is, Mary saw it coming. She saw how her son was offending the religious establishment. She saw a fickle crowd who didn't care about Jesus' well-being but only about what he could do for them. She saw that if something didn't change, her son's actions would lead directly to a nightmare.

So she tried to stop it, tried to intervene. But Jesus would not allow her to step between him and his eventual arrest. He called her to lay down her will, become a disciple, and in doing so, submit to God's will (see Matt. 12:50; Mark 3:35; Luke 8:21).

That choice would lead directly to *Gabbatha*, the place of judgment. It would lead to the very thing she most feared would happen. Because sometimes going in to Jesus, sitting at his feet, letting go of our expectations, submitting to him, leads us to the very place we don't want to go. He leads us to a place where we must face our worst fears.

Mary faced hers with the words "Crucify him!" Jesus had been arrested. He'd been shuffled back and forth between the Jewish council of chief priests, elders, and scribes, to the Roman governor Pilate, to Herod Antipas, and back to Pilate again.

And now he stood before the chief priests, crowds, and Romans — the religious leaders, the rabble, and the outsiders — representatives of all the world, and he was condemned to die.

This was Mary's worst fear, any mother's worst fear. But how much worse for her! From the beginning, she believed and she submitted, and when challenged, she chose discipleship over her own will. She pondered in her heart, had her expectations broken, and still believed.

So how could all of that lead her here?

Does God really, truly, make us face our worst fears?

Yes.

Yes, sometimes he does.

Hey, What about Prayer?

At any moment, things could have gone differently. Mary could have stayed home and found out about Jesus' crucifixion only after it occurred. But we know from John 19:26 that she was there. Jesus could have been released. We know from John 19:4–16 that Pilate wanted to release him. Even Herod found no guilt in him (Luke 23:13–15). And then there was the governor's custom of releasing a prisoner at the time of the Passover festival. Surely Jesus, an innocent man who a few days before was being hailed with cries of "Hosanna to the Son of David! Blessed is he who comes in the name of the Lord!" (Matt. 21:9) would be the one chosen to be set free.

But he wasn't.

Despite all the prayers from his disciples, his followers, those who cared—despite Mary's prayers—Jesus was not set free. Consider how desperately, how faithfully, she must have prayed for her son's release. She would have prayed when she first heard of his arrest.

But he was seized anyway.

She would have prayed when she knew he was meeting before Annas and Caiaphas.

But he was found guilty anyway.

She would have prayed when she heard that the whole council was judging him and false witnesses were accusing him. She would have prayed that they would see the truth and accept it.

They didn't.

She would have prayed when Jesus was in front of Pilate that even this Roman governor who was known for his cruelty would see her son's innocence and set him free.

He did … but he didn't.

She must have prayed when Jesus was sent to Herod that all her efforts to keep her son safe from another Herod, this Herod's father, would not be in vain. She must have prayed that Jesus would perform some miracle to delight Herod Antipas and the tetrarch would let him go.

But Jesus wouldn't. And Herod didn't.

When she heard Pilate mention the custom of setting a prisoner free at Passover, she might have believed that finally, finally, God was answering her prayer. Now, surely, Jesus would be released to continue his ministry, to become the Messiah-King she'd once sung about. Now God would move and this horror would end.

But he didn't. And it didn't.

Why?

No Other Way

Because this was the only way to accomplish God's will. Jesus had to die on a Roman cross for our sins so that we might be reconciled to God.

There was no other way.

Of course, Mary didn't know that. But God did. And so do we.

> The Messiah did not ascend to an earthly throne. He was anointed not with kingly oil but with his own blood.

We know that the Messiah had to die a sinner's death in our place that we might be free. From Jesus' prayer in the Garden of Gethsemane, we know that if there were an easier path, God would have chosen it. For Jesus prayed, "My Father, if it is possible, may this cup be taken from me" (Matt. 26:39).

And the soldiers, crowds, and Jewish leaders came and arrested him. They bound him. They beat him. They crucified him. And it was God's will.

There was no other way.

The Messiah did not ascend to an earthly throne. The religious leaders did not recognize him. He was rejected, and a crown not of gold but of thorns pressed upon his head, anointed not with kingly oil but with his own blood.

There was no other way.

Isaiah 53:3–6 says:

> *He was despised and rejected by mankind,*
> *a man of suffering, and familiar with pain.*
> *Like one from whom people hide their faces*
> *he was despised, and we held him in low esteem.*
> *Surely he took up our pain*
> *and bore our suffering, yet we considered him punished*
> *by God,*
> *stricken by him, and afflicted.*
> *But he was pierced for our transgressions,*
> *he was crushed for our iniquities; the punishment that*
> *brought us peace was on him,*
> *and by his wounds we are healed.*
> *We all, like sheep, have gone astray,*
> *each of us has turned to our own way; and the LORD*
> *has laid on him*
> *the iniquity of us all.*

He was sinless, and condemned. He was lied about, and the truth didn't prevail. He was accused, and said nothing. He was scourged, and not rescued. And then he died on a criminal's cross.

There was no other way.

"It was the LORD's will to crush him," says Isaiah 53:10. There was no other way for Jesus to satisfy his messiahship. No other way for the prophecies to be fulfilled. No other way for the promises to come true.

No easier way for Mary to become who she was always meant to be — not just the mother of the Messiah but the mother of the Savior.

"God allows us to experience the low points of life in order to teach us lessons that we could learn in no other way," says C. S. Lewis in *The Problem of Pain*.

The God who called Mary to face her worst fears is the same God who calls us. He calls in those times when the worst happens, when what we feared might happen does happen. When it seems that life has gone from bad to worse and every time we pray something even more awful happens, that is when God is saying to us: *There is no other way.*

No other way for him to accomplish his will in your life, to make you the person you were meant to be. If this cup could pass, it would.

But it doesn't.

Because this is the way. And sometimes we must walk in it, with faith, with trust, with one foot in front of the other, even when all our fears come true.

Who Is This God?

So who is this God who forces us to face our worst fears and refuses to answer our prayers to take this cup from us? Who is he whose will includes a Messiah's arrest, beating, and horrific death? Who is he who sends a mother to witness the death of her son?

This God is the one who takes us where we don't want to go to do what we never dreamed possible.

He is the God who says "Follow me!" in the midst of the worst times in our lives.

Will we say, "Your will be done … even if it's this nightmare," as we pray and sweat and bleed?

We are called by this God to face our fears and love anyway, follow anyway, believe anyway.

Unanswered Prayer?

Even when prayers are answered with only a resounding "No"?

Even when we pray and things get worse? Even when it seems like God hasn't heard us at all?

Yes.

After all, a lot of people in the Bible didn't get their prayers answered the way they wanted. But God's will was done anyway. Here is just a small sampling:

- **Jonah:** Jonah prayed to the Lord, "Isn't this what I said, Lord, when I was still at home? That is what I tried to forestall by fleeing to Tarshish" (Jonah 4:2).

  Jonah wanted Israel's enemies in the city of Nineveh to be destroyed. He prayed for Israel's freedom from the horror inflicted on them by the Assyrians (Nineveh was their capital city). Instead, God sent him to preach to them, to warn them what would happen if they didn't repent. Jonah fled in the opposite direction, toward Tarshish, to avoid the outcome he dreaded — the Ninevites repenting and being saved. But things got worse with a storm at sea and Jonah being swallowed by a huge fish then being vomited up on shore. Jonah went to Nineveh — the last place he ever wanted to go. He preached. They repented. And God did not destroy the city before Jonah's eyes. His enemies remained. Jonah's prayers weren't answered. The worst thing he imagined happened. But God's will was done.

- **Paul:** In 2 Corinthians 12:7 – 9, Paul said, "Therefore, in order to keep me from becoming conceited, I was given a thorn in my flesh, a messenger of Satan, to torment me. Three times I pleaded with the Lord to take it away from me. But he said to me, 'My grace is sufficient for you, for my power is made perfect in weakness.'"

  Three times Paul prays, and each time God answers with a resounding, "No!" But God's will is done. Paul's character is refined, and God's power is made perfect in Paul's weakness.

- **Jesus:** Matthew 26:36 – 46 records Jesus praying to his Father: "Then Jesus went with his disciples to a place called Gethsemane.... Then he said to them, 'My soul is overwhelmed with sorrow to the point of death....' Going a little farther, he fell with his face to the ground and prayed, 'My Father, if it is possible, may this cup be taken from me. Yet not as I will, but as you will.' ... He went away a second time and prayed, 'My Father, if it is not possible for this cup to be taken away unless I drink it, may your will be done.' ... He left them and went away once more and prayed the third time, saying the same thing. Then he returned to the disciples and said to them, '... Look, the hour has come, and the Son of Man is delivered into the hands of sinners. Rise! Let us go! Here comes my betrayer!'"

Jesus was barely done praying when the answer came in the form of the arresting party armed with swords and torches. One of Jesus' closest friends, Judas, was leading them and betrayed him with a sign of love, a kiss. Jesus was then beaten, mocked, and crucified. God, his Father, essentially said to his Son, "No! My will is not for this cup to pass. I will take you where you don't want to go, and you will accomplish what no one has thought possible." Jesus would accomplish the salvation of all who would believe on him for eternal life. Because God said no, Jesus went where he didn't want to go and faced a nightmare death.

The reason these men's prayers weren't answered in the way they'd hoped was not because God abandoned them or because God didn't love them or because they'd used a wrong prayer formula. It wasn't because they didn't have enough faith or had made God mad or weren't worthy.

Instead, it was because God was accomplishing his will not only for them *but for others around them*. God was up to something that required more faith, more trust, more submission to his will. God had another plan. Saying no to their prayers was the only way to accomplish that plan, God's vision, for them and for us.

God takes us where we don't want to go, just as he did Jonah, Paul, and Jesus, because he is doing something that is meant to glorify himself through our lives, meant to bless others through us. His vision is bigger than our comfort, more glorious than our need for health, happiness, satisfaction, or even earthly life. He is doing something more, something wondrous, something nearly unimaginable.

Going Where You Don't Want to Go

Jesus told Peter, "Very truly I tell you, when you were younger you dressed yourself and went where you wanted; but when you are old you will stretch out your hands, and someone else will dress you and lead you where you do not want to go." Jesus said this to indicate the kind of death by which Peter would glorify God. Then he said to him, "Follow me!" (John 21:18–19).

God's main concern isn't to make our nightmares go away. It's to build our character, teach us to trust him more fully, and help us to make a difference in the lives of those around us as we find the deep places of God in the dark places of life. God's will is that, by life or by death, we would glorify him.

So when he leads you where you don't want to go, remember he is with you. He loves you. He is working his will. Yes, even in the nightmares. Because there he is whispering to you, *There is no other way to make you into the person I created you to be. There is no other way to affect the lives of those around you.* "This is the way; walk in it" (Isa. 30:21).

Through fear, through terror, through every nightmare-come-true, God is saying, *Follow me!*

CHAPTER 12

He Still Cares

John's New Job

JOHN 19:25 – 27

❦

There is a tiny story tucked into the larger drama of the passion of Christ, a few verses mentioned only in the gospel of John. A little story that shakes me to my core. A moment amid all the blood and pain and dying when Jesus spoke but five words to his mother. Five words to a woman watching her Messiah-son die the most excruciating death possible. Five words that changed my life.

Jesus looked to his mother, then to his disciple, John, and said, "Woman, here is your son."

These are simple words, easy to pass over, but in them lies the answer to the deepest cries of my heart. Here, in one brief instant, Jesus answers my fears, assuages my doubts, whispers to me a divine truth.

In my darkest moments, in my despair, when all seems lost, these are the questions I ask: "Does he still care? Does he see me? Does he remember? Does he love?"

In these five words, Jesus tells me, "Yes!" He tells me he sees me, he remembers me, and yes, he still cares. In the midst of those moments when I can barely see beyond my tears, Jesus says, "I still love you. I love you from the cross."

For Mary it must have happened much like this:

Mary Tells Her Story

I am going on another journey with Jesus. But this one is not to Bethlehem or Egypt or even back to Jerusalem. This one is different from all the ones that have come before, because this time he is anything but safe. There is no stable awaiting us. There is no refuge in a far-off land. There is no circle of men impressed with the answers he gives. It's all over now. This is the final journey—the journey to a hill called Golgotha, the Place of the Skull.

A journey to death.

It is a short trip, and yet it seems to take an eternity to complete. Each step is agony. Each step brings us closer to the end of all hope.

They are making Jesus carry his own cross along the streets of the city. Just as Isaac carried the wood to the place of his sacrifice, so my son carries the wooden cross. But this time there will be no ram caught in the thickets. He is the ram. He is the lamb.

The crowds follow. They mock him. Some throw stones.

I weep.

He staggers on.

But he is too weak. His flesh hangs in tatters from the scourging. Blood dries on his temples from where the *akanthos* thorns have buried deep.

He stumbles. He falls. The cross crushes him to the ground.

I take a step toward him, but I cannot reach him. Cannot help him now.

It is too late.

Too late for us all.

What will we do now that hope goes to die? What will *I* do?

A soldier grabs a man from the crowd. "You there!" he shouts.

The burly man shrinks back. He does not want to come close to the beaten and bloody mess that is my son.

But the soldier jabs his finger toward the heavy beam that presses into my son's shoulders.

Slowly, so slowly, the man approaches. He lifts the beam, and together they inch forward to the Place of the Skull.

Step-by-step. Shaking, dragging the heavy cross.

I barely recognize the man my Jesus has become.

I can hardly see him through my tears.

But still I follow. I follow a trail of blood in the dirt.

His blood.

For a moment, I pause, kneel, and touch a trembling finger to a single drop in the dust.

His blood stains my skin, changes me. And I weep there, my tears mixing with the spatters of blood.

Ahead of me, he falls again.

I stand, stumble onward.

So does he.

Stumble, fall, stumble on. Fall again. Another step. Another tear. Another moment of unbelievable agony. For both of us.

And then we are there, at the death place. The large man, the Cyrene, drops the cross to the ground and melts into the crowd. Did he know that he carried the execution instrument of a King, of the very Son of God?

God, Father of my son, even now you could save him.

But he won't. Somehow I know that.

They lay the cross on the ground. They lay Jesus on the cross. They spread his arms wide.

I cannot bear to look.

But still I hear the echoing thud of the hammer hitting the spike. I hear his gasp.

And I feel the spikes piercing into my soul.

Simeon was right.

They strike again. Then pause.

I smell the blood, the sweat. Bile rises in my throat. The smell of his pain. The scent of filth in the crowds around me.

Evil pulses through the air.

The hammer falls again. I hear the clang of wood on metal. Again and again as the nails are driven deep.

My world tips, spins. I am on my knees. How did I get here? How did he?

I crawl forward.

Once more the hammer strikes.

His breath hisses. The crowds shift.

Someone touches my shoulder. I look up. My young nephew is there beside me, his eyes red with tears, his face pale.

"John."

He reaches out his hand. I take it. He pulls me to my feet, into his arms. His voice rattles in my ear. "We all ran. We didn't stay by him ... and now, now ..."

He cannot finish his words. But they echo in my ears and mix with the sound of the hammer's final blow.

My sister, Mary, appears beside me. And then another Mary, the one they call Magdalene, touches my elbow, looks deep into my eyes. I see her horror. It reflects my own.

We have no words. No words of greeting, no words of comfort, no words of hope.

Together we creep closer, closer. Closer to the place of death.

They lift him, his body hanging limp from the cross. Up, up, and then down as the cross thuds into the hole they made for it. They pack the dirt tight around the wooden base and step back.

The cross stands. I read the inscription of his guilt: THE KING OF THE JEWS.

We have rejected our King.

And Jesus, my son, my hope, my own Messiah-King, the one I love, hangs there between heaven and earth, between his Father and me. He is bleeding, dying, lifted up where I can't reach him, and his Father won't ... not anymore.

Two thieves are crucified beside him, one to his left, one to his right. He hangs in the midst of the sinners he so loved. Perhaps it is right that the company of sinners should surround him now. It means something, though at this moment, I don't know what. I can't understand.

So I stand here, at the foot of a Roman cross, watching my son's chest heave, smelling the sickly sweet scent of his shed blood, unable to do a single thing but weep.

Does he know I'm here? Does he know I would have changed all this if I could have? Does he know I still love him?

The crowds are jeering now, telling him to come down from the cross.

I wish he would. He is the only Son of God. He has the power. He could call down the angels of heaven to release him. He who healed others could heal himself in a moment. He could be shining, glorious, beautiful.

If only he'd come down from the cross. I want him to.

Or do I? What would it mean if he did what the crowds are demanding? What would it mean for me? For us all?

I shiver. "Jesus?"

He looks down at me.

And he sees me.

I reach my hand toward him.

"Woman," he says. A single word, spoken through blood, through pain, and in it, a memory of a time when he called me "woman" once before. I remember a wedding feast. I remember empty jars filled with water and turned to wine. I remember ...

But this is no wedding feast, is it?

And how will he now turn our water into his wine?

His eyes turn to John beside me. And he speaks to me a handful of simple words: "Behold, your son."

John touches my shoulder, moves closer, as Jesus speaks directly to him. "Behold, your mother!"

He does see. He does know.

He knows he will die.

There will be no miracle today.

Or will there?

Because even from a Roman cross, when all hope seems lost, he still cares for me.

The Wonder of Golgotha

Have you made your own journey to the Place of the Skull, to the place where hope itself is crucified and all you can see is death and fear and sorrow? Have you knelt there in the dirt, gripping the rocks in your hands, wondering how any good could ever come of this horror you're forced to endure?

Have you asked, "Does Jesus see me? Does he remember? Does he even care anymore?"

Have you asked, "Does Jesus see me? Does he remember? Does he even care anymore?"

I have. And so has my daughter Joelle. When her horse, Oreo, died, we were both asking those questions. And God answered. He showed us his care.

Joelle's Golgotha

Of course, for you and me, the death of a much-loved horse may seem trivial compared to Mary watching her son die on a Roman cross. But to a six-year-old girl, losing her black-and-white paint pony was a hurt that pierced more deeply than anything else she had ever experienced. And just as Jesus cared for Mary from the cross, so he also cared for Joelle when she faced her loss. There, at her little Golgotha moment, he was there. He cared. He loved. He ministered to her needs in ways that changed her and changed me.

Just a few months before Oreo's death, Joelle had made her very serious commitment-to-God-for-a-lifetime pledge and was eager to follow him, to believe, to trust. She had gone in, sat in the circle around Jesus' feet, and determined to be one who did the will of the Father—to be in Jesus' true family.

But when our vet glanced over the back of Joelle's growing-far-too-thin horse and said the dreaded word *cancer*, I knew we were in for heartbreak. I knew this was a path we didn't want to walk, would never choose to take. We were walking the path to death.

For over a month, we'd struggled to discover what was causing Oreo's decline. Exams and blood tests revealed nothing. Prayers for healing did nothing. She continued to lose weight. We continued to pray.

But now, with a single word from the vet, the sentence had been issued, and her body handed over to die.

Oh, Lord ... not Oreo.

Later I walked back into the house. Joelle met me at the door. "What did he say?"

"I'm sorry, honey. Oreo has cancer."

Her eyes dampened. "Is she going to die?"

I nodded as words stuck in my throat, refusing to be voiced.

Oreo, our perfect little horse. She'd taught Joelle to ride. Joelle had taught her to jump. They were a team, and Joelle loved her.

Tears streamed down my daughter's face. "But we prayed! How come God didn't make her better? But I want ... but she ..." She couldn't go on. Instead, she collapsed in my arms.

I patted her hair, thinking, *Here we go.* This was the first step of the journey to Joelle's Golgotha, a trip marked by sorrow but which would end in something we never dreamed. Just as it did for Mary, it would end with a new glimpse of Jesus.

For the next weeks, as Oreo continued to waste away, we watched, we loved, we cared, we prayed, and we kept on. We stumbled forward. So did Oreo.

We asked for hope. We asked for healing.

But God didn't heal Oreo. One day while my husband was away and my girls were at school, I found Oreo lying in her pen. I knew she would never get up again.

I waited, and I watched. And so did Oreo.

God gave that little horse the strength to hold on until Joelle got home from school.

We ran to her, gathered around her, held her, petted her, and told her how much we loved her. Joelle thanked her for being such a good horse and partner. We talked about heaven and being made new. Then we prayed.

For forty minutes, we stayed with her, with Joelle at her head, talking, praying, petting, holding, and crying. And God was with us. We felt him there, giving Oreo a last bit of life so we could say our good-byes, so we would know he cared. He wept with us.

Then Oreo gave one last shudder, stretched, and died there in our arms. As she passed, Joelle started to pray again. She thanked God for Oreo. She cried. She looked up into the sky and called out her final farewells. And in her prayers, through her sorrow, we glimpsed a bit of heaven. Somehow we saw the love of the Savior-come-to-earth, the same Savior who saw his mother and cared for her from the cross even as he was dying.

And we knew that even in sorrow, in death, God was loving us.

The next day, we put flowers on Oreo's grave and Joelle prayed such a sweet prayer of thankfulness that my heart broke all over again. She had made her commitment to belong to God, and now, so soon after, God sent her on this unwanted journey to Golgotha, deepening her faith and her vision of him, taking her from "Why?" to "Thank you," teaching her the secrets of gratefulness in pain.

Even now, years later, sometimes I see Joelle staring off with a serious look in her eye. Then I know she's thinking of her Oreo. And in those times, I know that she is remembering the final moments when God gave Oreo enough life for Joelle to get home and hold her horse, to pray, to find God in a new way at Golgotha.

Joelle is remembering that even in our saddest, most hopeless, fearful, and desperate moments, Jesus still cares. He loves us in the small things. He loves us from the cross.

Just like he loved Mary.

Mary's Golgotha

It's almost crazy when you think about it. After all, Jesus was dying. He'd been beaten, scourged, stripped, mocked, rejected. He'd had a crown of thorns crushed onto his head, spikes driven through his hands and feet. He was weak and bleeding.

And more. The sins of the whole world were being placed on him.

Yet, in the midst of all that, there was this tiny pause, this moment when Jesus saw his mother there at the foot of the cross and cared for her needs, gave her a new family. Scholar D. A. Carson says, "It is wonderful to remember that even as [Jesus] hung dying on a Roman cross, suffering as the Lamb of God, he took thought of and made provision for his mother.... Jesus displays his care for his mother as both she and the beloved disciple are passing through their darkest hour, on their way to full Christian faith."

But what a strange way to show care! Mary was in the midst of her nightmare-come-true. She was watching her Messiah-son die on a Roman cross. Her heart was breaking, her hope was shattered, her soul was pierced. I doubt very much that she was thinking, *Oh, who will take care of me now that my oldest son is dying?* That had to be the last thing on her mind.

But it was not the last thing on Jesus' mind.

Instead of offering comforting words to give hope, instead of reminding her of his promise to rise again, he assured her that, yes, he was going to die. In assigning her care to another, to John, he was confirming her worst fear, his imminent death.

A New Family

And yet Jesus was doing more. He was making absolutely sure that Mary would be cared for, her needs met. And he was placing the responsibility of that care into the hands of the disciple he loved. Jewish custom decreed that it was the oldest son's responsibility to care for his widowed mother. Normally that responsibility would then fall to the next son if the oldest were to die. But Jesus assigned John to that role. It is significant that John is described as "the disciple whom [Jesus] loved" in John 19:26.

First, this wording emphasizes that Jesus assigned the care of his mother not to a biological son but to one of his followers. In addition, we are reminded of Jesus' love for that disciple. The love that was given to John was now to be shared with Mary.

Furthermore, the formal way in which Jesus commended Mary's care to John emphasized that he was creating a new family for her. In the first century, a man who was being crucified had the right to make "testamentary dispositions" regarding his family and his possessions. Here Jesus used the official formula of Jewish family law to assign the care of his mother to John.

Jesus, from the cross, made sure that Mary was not just cared for physically but had a place in the family of God. He was not just assigning a caregiver for Mary; he was creating a new family. He was creating the church. Even today he joins his followers together through his love, makes them a new family, and lays on them the

Jesus joins his followers together through his love and lays on them the responsibility for caring for each other.

responsibility for caring for each other in his name. God cares. Jesus cares. Enough to give us a real family, the family of God.

That is part of the work that Jesus did from the cross. He did not leave his mother bereft. He didn't leave us bereft. Nor did he try to comfort her, or us, simply with reminders of a hopeful future. Instead, he did something concrete, something that demonstrated his care in the here and now.

In the midst of sorrow and pain, Jesus saw his mother, he loved her, and he created a new family for her, for us, just as he created fine wine out of plain water.

Remembering Water and Wine

Only in two places in the gospel of John does Jesus use the word "woman" when addressing his mother—here, from the cross, and in John 2:4 when he performs his first miracle at the wedding in Cana. I think we are meant to see the connections between the two incidents.

In John 2, Jesus shows attention to detail, calls Mary to be a disciple, creates something new in the face of emptiness, shame, and loss. Here Jesus again pays attention to the details of her true need, places her in a position with his disciples, and creates something new that meets the needs of all in the midst of sorrow, shame, and loss. He creates a new family.

In the moment of desperate need, when the wine is all gone, when hope is lost, Jesus sees Mary, he remembers, he cares, he creates.

From this we know that even in our deepest sorrow, our darkest pain, our most desperate, hopeless moments, Jesus is attending to the details of our lives. He is caring for us, loving us, calling the family of God to be the hands and feet and heart of his love.

He did that for Mary. For John. For you and me.

So when you have traveled to your own Golgotha, when you feel alone, forgotten, hopeless, and desperate, remember that Jesus sees you. He is caring for you. He is creating something new. He has prepared a new family for you.

And he is paying attention to the details. He has not forgotten, has not turned away.

He loves you—even from the cross. You are not alone. We are a family.

Who Is This God?

So, who is this God who pauses on the cross to care, to create ... for all of us? And more importantly, do I believe that's who he is? Do I really believe he cares for me, he loves me, when my world is falling apart and all hope seems lost?

Do I not only say I believe it, but do I live like I do?

I ponder this question, roll it over in my mind, in my heart. I sigh, lift my gaze from the computer screen, and stare out my office window.

What do I really believe?

Fog presses against the windowpane. Gray, bleak, blocking out the sun. On some days when I look out my window, I can almost glimpse eternity. It stretches down the green valley lined with oaks and touches the distant, snow-frosted mountains. On those days, I look out over the tall Monterey pines and search out that special place where sky meets earth in a blaze of blue glory. And I know that God is real, that he created all this beauty, and that he shares it with me because he loves me. On those days, I have no doubts, no questions, no fear. No Golgotha.

This day, however, is not one of those days. I can see no mountains, no valley. Even the tops of pines are blotted from my view. Instead, dark mist laces through the bottom branches and swirls in thick ripples across the ground. Grayness washes up to the window and forms tiny water droplets on the glass. It covers the mountains, masks the oaks, camouflages the pines.

And I know the fog won't lift today. And maybe not tomorrow. It could be days before I catch sight of the mountains or valley again. But the vision of snow-topped mountains and the deep green of the valley oaks remains fixed in my mind. I know the mountains are out there even though I can't see them. I trust that the trees remain green and beautiful even when they are lost to my sight.

As I sit and listen to the silence tangle with the fog outside, I am reminded of the Bible's definition of faith. Hebrews 11:1 says, "Now faith is confidence in what we hope for and assurance about what we do not see."

Even on Golgotha. Even at the foot of the cross. Even amid the fog.

I used to live as if faith was seeing the mountains. I believed that if I only had enough faith, I would see God clearly; I would always know what he wanted; I wouldn't have any doubts, any questions. There would never be any fog.

But these days, I see faith differently. Faith, I've come to believe, doesn't dispel the fog but is found within it. Faith isn't about seeing the mountains. It's about believing they are there when all my senses deny it. It's about believing in that spot of blue glory when all I see is the persistent grayness.

There are times when nothing makes sense, when hurt and confusion press against the window of my soul, when doubts creep in and twine around my thoughts as surely as the fog twists through the trees. There are times when God seems to hang between heaven and earth and I crumble on the laundry room floor and wonder if God really loves me.

That's when faith flourishes. As surely as I can say I know the mountains and oaks and pines are there, even though I can't see them, so I can say that I know God loves me even though I can't see it now. I know that I am his and that he loves me from the cross. I choose to believe what I cannot see. For faith is not seeing but believing, even in the fog. *Especially* in the fog.

It is remembering that moment on the cross when Jesus looks down and cares, deeply, intimately, and creates a new thing in the midst of pain. It is knowing that this is the God who is Love, in the big things *and* in the little things.

This is the God who made garments for Adam and Eve after they sinned (Gen. 3:21). He is the God who provided manna in the wilderness (Ex. 16), who sent ravens to feed Elijah when he was hiding in Kerith Ravine (1 Kings 17:3 – 4), who made water turn to wine at a wedding feast.

He is the God who provides for your needs even when all seems lost.

He is the God who creates a new family, his church.

So, when circumstances are desperate, when you feel all alone, when death drips on the rocky ground and calls the name of one you love, Jesus sees you. He remembers you. And he is caring for you in the details of your life.

Woman, he says, *behold your son.*

You are not forgotten. You are loved.

I will turn your water to wine ... even now.

By my blood, I have made you a part of the family of God.

CHAPTER 13

In the Dark

At the Foot of the Cross

LUKE 23:44–45

❦

I love the book of Job. But sometimes, well, it scares me. Verses like this make me tremble:

Have the gates of death been shown to you?
Have you seen the gates of the deepest darkness? (Job 38:17)

I read God's questions to Job and shudder. *The gates of deepest darkness?* No one wants to be shown those. We cringe from darkness. We flip light switches, turn on nightlights, light candles, switch on lamps until all the corners of our lives are illuminated with artificial light.

We beat back the shadows. We deny the dark.

And we pretend. We pretend there is no darkness, no moments that are not filled with God's light.

At least I do.

And yet God is not absent in the darkness. He is found even there. And he is working even when we don't perceive him. It is in the darkness that God does his most intimate work in us.

Mary taught me that. She was there in a darkness where Jesus could no longer be seen. She was there when the noonday sun failed and her world was swallowed by black, when the curtain in the temple was torn in two from top to bottom, when the ground shook with the magnitude of the moment that changed everything.

God is working even when we don't perceive him. It is in the darkness that God does his most intimate work in us.

And she faced the questions that haunt us all: Where is God when the world goes dark, when you can't see him, when the earth shakes? What is he doing? What does it mean?

And how could it be that it is in the darkness that the promises come true?

When you can't see him, when you don't understand — there he is rending the curtain. He is opening the Holy of Holies to you, to me ... to Mary.

Perhaps it happened something like this:

Mary Tells Her Story

He will not come down. My son will not come down from this wooden cross, from the thing that will kill him. He hangs there, and there is nothing I can do to change it now.

He will die.

I will cry.

And struggle to understand the inexplicable.

The sun is at its zenith now. In the fullness of its strength, it beats down on me. I kneel here on the rocky earth. I squeeze the dirt in my hands. Sweat trickles down my back.

And I wait.

For something. For anything that will ease my pain. Ease his.

Nothing does.

He bleeds.

I wait.

He groans.

I weep.

God in heaven, where have you gone? Do you not see? Do you not hear? Will you do nothing as our son dies here beneath the sun?

I whisper the words. I await his response.

And then something strange, something impossible, happens. The sky turns dark. Not just from a passing cloud but black like night. Black, at noonday.

I stand and shiver in the blackness. Those around me cry out. I hear the shuffle of their feet. A gasp. A scream. A keening wail.

"What's happening?" someone shouts.

"God has come to judge us," yells another.

Is this the answer of God? At Jesus' birth, we were bathed in dazzling light. At his death, we are covered in unnatural darkness.

The sun itself has failed.

Will my faith fail too?

I remember the prophet Amos who said, " 'In that day,' declares the Sovereign LORD, 'I will make the sun go down at noon and darken the earth in broad daylight.... I will make that time like mourning for an only son.' "

A time of mourning.

It has come true. Today God keeps the promise of our pain.

The darkness remains, lies heavily upon us. Someone bumps against me. Another touches my arm. I put my hand in front of my face and cannot see the trembling fingers, cannot glimpse my own dirty palms. I hear the harsh breathing of those around me, but I cannot see their faces. Not now. Not anymore.

My world has turned black as pitch.

I hear the clank of metal from a guard's uniform, the now-hushed whispers of the crowd.

They are afraid. And so am I.

I cannot see. Cannot understand. I can't see God. I can't see my son.

I hear a sizzle in the darkness. Then a single torch flares to life. Beneath it, I see a Roman face. A guard with his helmet low on his brow. The light shimmers off beads of sweat, illuminating them like a sheen of tears. He lifts the torch higher. Almost I can see the feet of my Messiah-son in its glow.

Almost.

The wind blows sand across my face, flickers the flame of the torch. Suddenly even it is snuffed.

A crucified thief cries out. The clatter of hooves. Panicked cries. The patter of retreating feet. And the quiet dripping of my son's blood on the rocks before me.

Hours pass. And still there is only the darkness. The deep blackness as if God himself refuses to see.

Darkness. And somewhere in it, my son. Dying in the dark.

I tremble. The ground quakes.

God, is there any meaning in this blackness?

Wonder in the Darkness

There is. There is meaning in the darkness, and more. Mary couldn't know it as she knelt at the foot of the cross, but she would see it later. She would understand when she was told that far away in the innermost temple, the curtain that separated her from the Holy of Holies was being torn in two.

She would understand, and we will, too, that in our darkness, when we don't see God, when we feel abandoned, when it seems that God has turned away, that is when he is tearing the curtain from top to bottom. He is opening the way to experience him, to know him, with far more intimacy than we ever dreamed possible.

> *When it seems that God has turned away, that is when he is opening the way to know him.*

In the darkness, God is working.

I know all this because I learned it in the dark. I learned it the hard way. I've been to the hilltop where I looked out on life and saw the breathtaking wonder of God in my life and saw it shimmering with nothing but joy. And I've been to the valley, to the deep, dark places, where I could not see at all, where Jesus was unrecognizable, where my hopes lay in tattered ruins at my feet and I didn't know if I'd ever find a way to believe again.

I know what it's like to look for God and see only shadows, to choke on songs of praise that I once sang so easily, to sit in a crumbled heap with the bits of my belief slipping through trembling hands.

I know what it's like to know all the right things, to proclaim them, and still wail in the blackness.

I am blessed, but often it doesn't feel like it. I am chosen, but I wonder, *For what? For this? How could it be for this?*

It took six miscarriages, twenty years of dealing with infertility, a failed church plant, and the many challenges of ministry to convince me that God does love me, that he does have a plan, and that it is in the darkness itself, the darkness I so rail against, that God does his most intimate work in me. It is there that he breaks down the barriers between us. It is there, when I can't see him at all, that he is nearest.

I discovered that one day while kneeling by the closet floor.

Sitting in the Dark

I pulled out a bag of baby clothes from the closet. I opened it, touched a tiny pink onesie, ran my fingers over a pair of itty-bitty shoes. I closed the bag and set it aside. My hands curled into fists.

God, I can't do this. It makes it so, so final.

I reached for another bag. A dozen little footie pajamas. A rattle. A stack of receiving blankets all clean and folded and ready for the new baby I knew we would never have.

That hope, that dream had died with our final miscarriage. And now—well, now there was nothing left but darkness, and bag after bag of baby clothes. I pulled each plastic bag from the closet. I pulled out a travel swing, a nursing pillow, a little knit hat.

I pulled out a closetful of baby things and heaped them in the middle of the room. A closetful of things that now represented nothing but pain and prayers gone unanswered. We were supposed to have a new baby. I was supposed to dress her in that onesie, wrap her in that blanket. She would have loved the swing. I could almost see her tiny face nuzzled against me on the nursing pillow.

But all that was over now. There would be no new baby. Death had come instead.

Death in the form of four final miscarriages and the end of all our attempts for another child.

Now the shoes and swings, pjs and pillows would be for the crisis pregnancy center. They would be for babies I would never know, never see.

I sat there, in my heap, and wept over all the hopes that had crumbled, all the dreams that had come to nothing, all the babies that had died in me before they ever had a chance to wear a onesie and put on teeny-tiny shoes.

I sat in my darkness. I cried out in anger. I cried with sorrow. My heart's hands beat on the chest of a God I couldn't see and didn't understand.

God, is any of it true? Any of those promises you gave in the Bible?

They say, "Jesus loves you." Well, I don't believe it. I can't. They talk of purpose. And I can't see any point to this awfulness. They say to trust. I don't know how. I thought you were saying there would be another baby, maybe two. Instead, there were only miscarriages. It doesn't make sense.

I stuffed a tiny bib back into a bag.

None of this makes sense.

But the end had come. Come unexpected and unwanted. Come despite all the promises I had read and believed in.

God, I am so mad I could spit. I am so sad I could cry forever. Where are you? Are you even out there? Why have you left me all alone?

How can you say you love me then leave me like this? Leave me in the utter darkness.

I wept, I railed, I accused, I cried out to a God I couldn't see, couldn't understand … and couldn't believe still loved me.

But he did.

Because in that moment of brokenness, of blackness, of my shaking, quaking faith, God was working. I wouldn't see it then. But I would see it in the weeks and months to come. I would get a glimpse when I dropped off the bags of baby clothes at the pregnancy center. I would see it more clearly when I started talking to women all around the world about infertility and miscarriage. And I would finally believe it when I converted the would-be nursery into a room for quiet reading and prayer.

Then I would know that in my time of darkness, God was breaking the barriers in me that kept me from knowing him more fully. He was ripping the curtain made of my expectations, of my own dreams, of my dependence on happiness to prove to me his love.

In my darkness, when I thought God had abandoned me, he was instead freeing me from wrong perceptions, an inadequate vision, a puny faith.

I sat on that bedroom floor as a woman who expected God to make her dreams come true. I would leave it as a woman who would come to see God not as her Santa in the sky but as a Father who cared more about his daughter's character than he did her happiness.

In the darkness, I was changed. I don't know how. And I can't explain it. But I do know that somehow, in my darkest moments, while I fumbled around in the blackness of my sorrow, anger, and doubts, God was in the process of ripping away the veil and revealing himself to me.

> *In my darkest moments, God was in the process of ripping away the veil and revealing himself to me.*

Now I look back on those years of infertility, on the six miscarriages, on the morning when I gathered all the baby bags and believed hope had died. I look back on the dark times and see that I am a different person for having gone through them. I see God like I never could have before those times. I know him in ways I never could have imagined. And while I still dread the darkness, I now know that I am not alone in it.

God is there. He is at work. He loves me even there in the dark, especially there when I can't see him.

He loves me.

Just as he loved Mary.

Darkness and the Curtain

When Jesus was on the cross, darkness covered the land for three hours, from noon until three in the afternoon. Commentators argue about what the darkness symbolized. It may have been meant to show that nature itself was mourning; it may have served as a sign of judgment; or it may even have been a way to say that the sun itself could not look upon the travesty of the Messiah's death. Some claim it showed the power of Satan over those moments.

But for those of us who have knelt in our own darkness, the arguments don't matter. Like Mary, we care little what the darkness symbolizes. It only matters that it is there, that we must live through it, live in it. We know that darkness means confusion and fear, sorrow and loneliness. This is a time when we can't see, we don't understand. It's when things are not as they should be, when life is turned upside down and nothing makes sense.

Commentator John Nolland says, "When the sun should have been at the height of its powers, instead darkness descended." Darkness came when there should have been light.

That is the kind of backwards, doesn't-make-sense, where-are-you-God moment that Mary and everyone around her experienced.

I've experienced it too. You probably have as well. We've been to the place where we can't seem to see any light at all. Mary couldn't see Jesus. We can't see God. Mary saw no comforting visions, no glimpses of God's light. She could do nothing but wait. We can do nothing but trust … or not. We choose.

Because for us, like Mary, we often don't know what is happening, what God is doing when we can't see him.

Luke 23:44–45 tells us, "It was now about noon, and darkness came over the whole land until three in the afternoon, for the sun stopped shining. And the curtain of the temple was torn in two."

Something was happening in the darkness.

Far away from where Mary was standing (or sitting or kneeling), something important was happening in the temple. In the darkness, the curtain that separated the people from the Holy of Holies was being torn in two. Luke clearly links the two events in the text. "The translation links the tearing of the veil to the sun's light failing (expressed by a genitive absolute)," says David Garland.

God is in the darkness. He is working. He is tearing the veil.

And this veil that was ripped asunder was no puny bit of muslin. It was a whole handbreadth thick. It was forty cubits long and twenty wide (sixty feet by thirty feet). It did not tear easily.

Woven from costly yarns from Babylon, the curtain blocked access to the Holy of Holies where the inner altar stood. Only once a year would the high priest enter through the curtain to make an offering for his sins and the sins of the people. That's how unapproachable, how separate, God was to the people.

But not forever. Because in the darkness, God was doing a new thing. In the Greek, the passive voice is used to describe the tearing of the curtain, showing us that God himself did the rending.

So what does it truly mean that God tears the veil?

In general, culturally then and now, the purpose of a veil is to cover, to separate. Brides wear veils as they walk down the aisle so the groom can't see them. Middle Eastern women wear veils to hide their faces from men.

This veil, this curtain, was to separate a holy God from a sinful people. But while Mary sat in the blackness, unable to see Jesus, unable to see God, God rent that veil in two. He removed the barrier. And he did it in the darkness.

So what does this tell us about our God? It says that no matter how deep our darkness, no matter the horror we face in it, God is there. He is working. He is, in fact, doing his most intimate work. God rends the curtain and reveals himself, takes down barriers, does a new thing, *in our darkest moments*. The curtains in your soul may be thick. They may be difficult to tear away. But our God knows how to rip through the thickest of veils. He has done it before. He will do it again. For you.

So what do we do when we face the darkness? Like Mary, we sit at the foot of the cross. We don't panic. We don't run away. Instead, we stay there, sit quietly, and let God work even though we can't see him.

Now, because of Christ, because of what he did on the cross for us, darkness is no longer the place where evil has its way. It is not the devil's realm. Instead, it has become the place where God works, where he comes near to us in new ways.

God is God, even in our darkness.

There he loves us. There he fulfills his purposes. There the promises of the Messiah come true because he is removing the separation between God and man. Between you and the God who loves you.

He is near us in the dark. He is opening the Most Holy Place. We must only trust, even when we cannot see.

> *Therefore, brothers and sisters, since we have confidence to enter the Most Holy Place by the blood of Jesus, by a new and living way opened for us through the curtain, that is, his body, and since we have a great priest over the house of God, let us draw near to God with a sincere heart and with the full assurance that faith brings, having our hearts sprinkled to cleanse us from a guilty conscience and having our bodies washed with pure water. Let us hold unswervingly to the hope we profess, for he who promised is faithful. (Heb. 10:19–23)*

Who Is This God?

Who is this God who splits curtains in the darkness? Who is he when we can't see him and don't know he's there?

God is the promise keeper and veil breaker. He is the one who transforms the darkness.

God calls us into a deeper relationship with him when the darkness is at its deepest. He calls us to remember his promises.

He calls us into a deeper relationship with him, into the Holy of Holies, when the darkness is at its deepest. He calls us to remember his promises and see what they really mean.

He calls us to himself.

Often we read our Bibles, quote the promises we find there, write them on social media walls. And what we mean by them is that God will step into our lives and make everything go well. There will always be light. We'll lead a charmed life where everything goes the way we want it to; we're successful, honored, loved, and blessed.

Except Jesus has redefined blessed. And sometimes the promises don't mean what we think they do. They mean something deeper, more wondrous. They are promises fulfilled in the darkness, made real in times we don't see the light.

Consider, as a small sampling, these oft-quoted promises from God in the New Testament:

Scripture says: "We know that in all things God works for the good of those who love him, who have been called according to his purpose" (Rom. 8:28).

What we hear: Only good things will happen to us as long as we're faithful. God will make our lives good and wonderful and easy.

What it really means: All the things that happen in our lives are not necessarily good, but God can transform the hard, difficult, hurtful, painful things for our good. Nothing is beyond his reach. Nothing surprises him. So, even though hard, horrible things will happen, he who transformed death itself can transform the hurtful things in our lives too. He can make them into something that changes us for the good. Though all will not be sunshine and roses, when hard times come, all is not lost, because even in the pain, God is working for our good. Trust him in the darkness.

Scripture says: "How much more will your Father in heaven give good gifts to those who ask him!" (Matt. 7:11).

What we hear: All we have to do is ask, and God will fill our lives with enough success, enough money, enough love, enough stuff to make us happy.

What it really means: God's gifts in our lives are good. Even the ones we're afraid of, the ones we hate, the ones we can't believe come from him. Sometimes his gifts are those of the "blessing" of Mary—suffering, loss, pain, and a life that doesn't go as planned. The tears are gifts from God too. Trust that the gifts are good even when they don't seem like it.

Scripture says: "My yoke is easy and my burden is light" (Matt. 11:30), because "He who did not spare his own Son, but gave him up for us all—how will he not also, along with him, graciously give us all things?" (Rom. 8:32).

What we hear: If we just walk with God, life will be easy. God will give us everything we need.

What it really means: His yoke is light, but that doesn't mean life is easy. We pick up our cross daily. We follow him. That cross we carry *is* the yoke that connects us to Jesus. And as we are yoked with him, he carries the weight and we learn what it means to be like Christ. We work, we pull the plow, we walk alongside the one who never had it easy. Because God really does give us all things, all things that are of Christ. And that includes suffering. It includes pain. It includes darkness. It includes things we don't expect and don't always understand. We receive all the riches of heaven and a taste of the suffering that will make us like him ... if we let it.

Scripture says: "With God all things are possible" (Matt. 19:26).

What we hear: God can and will do what I want.

What it means: Anything really is possible—even a Savior born in a barn, a Messiah dead on a cross, a life full of disappointment and pain but that still glorifies him ... Mary's life. And maybe yours. God can make you into the beautiful vision that he created you to be, but the path to get there must go through darkness.

Scripture says: "You may ask me for anything in my name, and I will do it" (John 14:14) and "Everyone who asks receives; the one who seeks finds; and to the one who knocks, the door will be opened" (Luke 11:10).

What we hear: If I just pray hard enough, if I use the right words, if I have the right prayer formula, then God will make my life just like I want it. He'll answer all my prayers.

What it really means: Ask, pray, hope, believe. But only the things you ask in his will—those things that represent Christ and what he wants for you and for those around you—will be answered with a "yes." And sometimes even those won't look as you expect. Remember that what he wants is rarely your ease, your comfort, your happiness. What he wants is for you to become the glorious vision of who he created you to be. He wants you to become a reflection of his glory. So ask, seek, knock … but don't think the answers you find when the door opens will be all happiness and light. The door will open. And he will be there. But this Messiah is more, so much more than you ever imagined …

He is the one who tears curtains in the darkness. He is the one who cares for you even from the cross. He hangs there, in the dark, to make all the promises true.

Even now, even here, even when it appears that nothing will be right again. Even when you can't see him. Even when it seems he's not there at all.

Here is where he loves you with an everlasting love.

Kneel at the foot of the cross, and know that he is doing his most intimate work in you; here, in the dark, the promises are coming true.

CHAPTER 14

Breaking and Remaking

It Is Finished

LUKE 23:46; JOHN 19:30

D^{eath.} I tremble as I type the word.

Death.

We've all tasted its bitter fruit. Death of a loved one, death of a dream, death of a relationship ... the death of our hopes and the promises of a bright future.

With Mary, we've all knelt at the foot of a cross. We've all wept and shuddered, knowing death has come near.

And then death arrives.

It is finished.

And yet God has only just begun to change the world, our world. He has only begun to change us. And we discover that death is not the end we once believed. It is but a doorway to the transformation of our souls.

Mary could not have seen it from

> *We discover that death is not the end we once believed. It is but a doorway to the transformation of our souls.*

218

where she knelt on Golgotha. She could not have known as she looked up at her dead son, as she experienced the worst moment of her life, that this very moment would change everything. It was the moment of inexplicable glory.

When all was lost ... all was saved. You were saved, I was saved, Mary herself was saved from all her sins. This was the moment God broke through and accomplished the most amazing, wondrous, beautiful thing of all time.

Her worst moment.

His death.

The moment of amazing wonder.

How could it be? For Mary it might have happened something like this:

Mary Tells Her Story

I never would have dreamed that a journey that began with a declaration of God's favor would end here, at the foot of a Roman cross. I could not have imagined this pain. I could not have envisioned the cruelty of the cross, the horror, the soul-rending sorrow of this impossible ending to a dream, a promise.

Yet here I am. Here he is.

And I don't understand it.

What is God's favor if it leads to a cross, if it brings me to the place of sorrow, of loss, of darkness? Of death?

What is God's favor if my prayers go unanswered, if the darkness never lifts, if there is only death and despair?

Who is this God who lets our son die and does nothing?

Will every dream, every hope, every promise of Messiah die with him?

The ground trembles beneath me. The wood of the cross creaks. The crowds gasp and groan. So do the thieves.

But not my Jesus.

He is silent now. Except for the hissing, rattling breath of a man about to die.

I fall to my knees. Stones jab into my skin. I wrap my arms around me. I am cold, so cold. Pain squeezes my chest.

Lord ... no.

It is near now. The end has come. I can sense it, almost smell it here in the dark. It smells of blood and sweat, of dirt and fear. It smells like the death of a Messiah.

Like the death of all my hopes.

God ... oh, God ...

I can't even pray. Not anymore.

Then a cry pierces the air, pierces my heart. His cry, loud and fierce.

"Father, into your hands I commit my spirit."

The darkness shudders.

Silence falls.

And in it, a whisper from above me: *It is finished.*

Finished.

The darkness breaks. The sun shines again. The glow hurts my eyes, stabs to my soul.

And there he is, my son, dead on the cross above me. Dead, with blood-stained nails through his hands and feet. Dead.

I remember an angel. I remember a baby born in a barn. I remember a son in the temple. I remember his laughter, the way his eyes would twinkle at a joke. I remember the warmth of his touch, the wisdom of his words. I remember the challenge in his voice as he called me to be more than a mother. He called me to be his disciple.

I remember my son, God's Son, the Messiah.

It seems that just yesterday he was only a boy with curly hair, his front teeth missing, a scratch on his elbow and dirt on his knees. Yesterday I held him in my arms and kissed his baby brow. Yesterday he lived. And hope lived with him.

Today my son is dead.

It is finished.

Nothing will ever be the same again.

Wonder in Becoming

There's something strange, eerie, about facing the death of someone who should not have died. It's one thing to watch an elderly loved one slip away after a long illness. It's quite another to face the death of someone who is young.

How do we believe in love in the face of death? How do we trust?

For both we grieve, we weep, we tremble in our sorrow. But when a child dies in the darkness, when there's nothing we can do to stop it, when all the promise of that life dies, we are left with even more than sorrow.

We are left with questions, doubts, and the stinging fear that perhaps, in this moment, God's love has failed us after all.

How do we believe in love in the face of death? How do we trust? How do we become the people God has created us to be?

I thought about these questions as I sat in the long wooden pew in a church in Santa Cruz, California. Light splashed through the stained-glass windows around me. People dressed in somber black lined the pews. A group of young women huddled behind me. To the left, a young man sniffed and fought not to cry. A woman dabbed her eyes. A baby wailed then grew silent. Music dwindled.

I glanced down at the paper in my hand. And I saw her face.

Sara. Bright eyes peeking over sunglasses, a mischievous half smile, filled with the promise of tomorrow. A young face. Too young to be printed on the program for a memorial service. Too young to be the cause of mourners dressed in black. Twenty-two years old. Too young to die.

I'd known her since she was a baby. Her parents attended the small Nazarene church in Palo Alto that my husband and I started attending in our last year at Stanford. They had come to our wedding, they had stayed in contact as we moved back and forth across the country in our early years of marriage. Then, when we started a church out of our home in Gilroy, they had traveled from another city to join us every Sunday. I had seen Sara grow from a toddler to a beautiful young teen, to a young woman.

A young woman who would take her own life.

The microphone crackled as one of Sara's friends stood up to share her memories of Sara. She sniffed and rubbed her cheeks. Her voice wavered. My throat clogged. And then, as she continued her story of Sara and their school days, I snuck a peek at Sara's parents. They sat on the other side of the church in the front pew. They sat with their faces forward, their shoulders touching, their hands clasped.

Tears filled my eyes. *These are the worst days of their lives.* I fumbled for the box of tissue beside me. To lose a full-grown daughter ... even I, then the mother of four young girls, couldn't imagine it. Or at least I didn't want to imagine. It hurt too much. It was hard enough to sit there in the pew remembering Sara—a little girl clinging to her mother's knees, a young teen flipping the pages in her Bible, an older teen sharing her poetry, a girl whom I'd known and prayed for almost all of her life.

Now she was gone, and her mother, my friend, sat there white-faced in the front pew, listening as others came forward and shared their memories of Sara, as the music played, as the pastor spoke words of God's love.

God's love.

It all seemed so unreal, so strange, so awful. God's love. I couldn't imagine that either. Not here. Not now. Not with Sara's mom, Noreene, sitting there in that pew with her face washed in sorrow. Where was God's love in something like this? Where was his care?

But then something happened. Something I will never forget.

As the final person to share memories of Sara finished, Noreene rose. She walked to the microphone. And she raised her hands toward heaven.

Then that mother whose heart had been broken with the loss of her only daughter prayed a prayer of thanksgiving. No "whys," no accusations, no questions of how God could have allowed such a thing to happen. Instead, with hands and eyes lifted, she thanked God for the gift of Sara's life, she thanked him for everything Sara had taught her about God's love and love for others, she praised him through the deepest part of her pain.

And she meant every word.

So I sat there and witnessed the beauty of faith of a beloved child of God. I saw what it meant to give thanks in all circumstances (1 Thess. 5:18), even in the hardest and most painful circumstance I could imagine. I saw a real woman of faith. And through her, I beheld the face of God. And it was the face of love.

That day, Sara's mom was transformed, and so was I. Through sorrow, through pain, through death.

There was a moment of becoming … becoming a little more of who she, of who I, was meant to be. There, surrounded by the reality of death, the darkness lifted … and I saw the horror of that death and the wonder of God. And I knew that somehow in the midst of the most painful thing I could imagine, God had revealed a glimpse of his glory and I would never, ever, be the same again.

Mary wouldn't either. In the face of the death of her child, Mary, too, experienced that moment of becoming. The moment of death, horror, sorrow, fear was also the moment of a wonder beyond anything she could have imagined, anything she had ever dreamed.

Mary's Dream

Because Mary had a dream. She had a hope. She had a promise.

Once, long ago, the angel had called her favored. He'd said the Lord was with her. And he'd given her promises for this Son who now hung dead on a cross.

The angel Gabriel had said:

- He will be great.
- He will be called the Son of the Most High.
- God will give him the throne of David.
- He will reign over Israel forever, and his kingdom will have no end. (Luke 1:28–33)

But now Jesus was dead.

He had been mocked, spat on, whipped, and called names that didn't include Son of the Most High. His only throne was a cross. And forever had ended in death.

Or so it seemed.

Once, long ago, Elizabeth had declared her the most blessed of all women. And Mary had sung with wondrous joy:

- All generations will call me blessed.
- The Mighty One has done great things for me.
- His mercy extends to those who fear him through all generations.
- He has performed mighty deeds.
- He scattered the proud and brought down rulers.
- He lifted up the humble and filled the hungry.
- He sent the rich away empty and helped Israel.
- He remembered to be merciful.

- Just as he promised.... Just as he always promised. (Luke 1:46–55)

But Jesus was dead. And God, his Father, let him die.

Mary seemed anything but blessed. What kind of blessing sends a mother to watch her firstborn son die on a Roman cross?

Where were the great things of God now? Where were his mercy and his mighty deeds? The proud were not scattered but gathered around him, mocking. The rulers still sat on their thrones. They were the ones who condemned him. God had indeed lifted up the humble ... lifted him up on a wooden cross.

And now, it was finished.

Can you imagine it? Watching your son arrested, beaten, spat on, and then nailed to a cross to die? The son you loved, the one you nursed and tickled, the one you cuddled, whose boo-boos you kissed. The one for whom you gave up all your plans and your former dreams to bear and to raise. The one who was supposed to make all things right again.

Can you imagine what it was like to watch him die?

Where was mercy? Where was favor? Where was blessedness? Where were all those promises now?

They were fulfilled.

Fulfilled! In ways Mary never could have dreamed, never would have expected.

That is the strange dichotomy of the cross, and of our lives. At the cross, in Jesus' death, the promises all came true. Here, when Mary was crushed, was the moment when God was doing something so astounding, so wondrous, that she never could have imagined it.

In the moment that encapsulated the very epitome of what it means for plans and hopes to go awry, to die, God performed the most wondrous, breathtaking act of all time. It was the moment of redemption, of glory, of splendor, of the answer to all the prayers

In the moment that held the epitome of what it means for plans and hopes to go awry, God performed the most wondrous act of all time.

and hopes from the beginning of time. It was that moment that purchased salvation for all humankind.

Jesus cried, "It is finished!" In the Greek, John used the perfect tense to show that it was completed, for all time, forever, perfectly whole and finished. Christ had finished the work he was sent to do. He had, in that moment, redeemed us all. Forever.

In the worst moment of her life, when God seemed absent, when all hope had died, God did his most glorious work.

Commentator R. Kent Hughes relates this story:

A small boy was turning the pages of a book of religious art. When he came to a picture of the Crucifixion he looked at it for a long time, and a sad look came to his face. Finally, he said, "If God had been there, he wouldn't have let them do it." So the Crucifixion seems—until we understand what it really meant. Then we learn that God was there on the cross. We learn that he willed it. We learn that because of the cross, grace flashed in the lives of Simon the Cyrenian, the daughters of Jerusalem, the crucifying soldiers, the thief, the centurion— and thousands upon thousands since that day.

Because of the cross, grace flashed into the life of Mary herself. Yes, the precise moment when all Mary's hopes died, when all her plans came to nothing, became the moment of answer. Because of the cross, all generations have called her blessed. At the cross, the Mighty One did the greatest thing he could have done for us: he died for us. Through the cross, his mercy extended to all generations. It was his mighty deed that scattered the proud, lifted the humble, filled the hungry, helped Israel and all the world. In the cross alone do we find ultimate mercy. Just as he promised. Just as he always promised.

I think it may often be that way for us as well. That there—at the very place where our dreams don't come true, where our hopes are shattered, where all we see is death—is where God is standing in the greatest power. Those are the moments, the places that change the world, where we find a depth and wonder deeper than we ever dared to dream.

Who She Was Meant to Be

But even more, these are the places where we are remade into the people God means us to be. Mary was meant to be the mother of the Savior. That was the call of the angel, the affirmation of Elizabeth, the blessing of Simeon. She was not called to be just the mother of a babe born without a human father. She wasn't to be just the mother of a good teacher, a righteous man, an earthly king. She was not meant to be simply the mother of one who would follow in David's line. Even the name Jesus means "God saves." But to fulfill the promises, Jesus had to die. In order for Mary to become the mother of our Savior, *Jesus had to die.*

It was the crucifixion that transformed her into who she was meant to be—the mother of the one who would save not just Israel but all who believed on him from every nation. He would save us not just from human enemies, foreign nations, and oppressors but from ourselves and our sin. He would reconcile us to God forever.

Through the cross. Through death. Through the most horrific moment of Mary's life.

Without dying, Jesus would be no savior. And Mary would never have been who she was called and created to be.

And this horror, this cross that bore her dead son, was the only way to her becoming the mother of the Savior of all humankind.

She became who she was meant to be.

She was transformed.

She was favored ... by becoming.

She was blessed ... by becoming.

Because that's what favor means. That's what true blessedness is: becoming who God created you to be. But that becoming will involve disappointment, pain, and the shattering of all your expectations and hopes — just as it did for Mary.

God has a dream, a vision, for you too. And to realize that vision, often we, too, must go through hardship, pain, and disappointment. We, too, must look into the face of the death of all our hopes. In your life, the death of plans, a relationship, a job, or even a person can also be the moment God's glory breaks through in ways you never dreamed. At the cross, we are called to look at death and see the hand of God. We are called to see ... and be amazed. Just like Noreene. In the face of her worst moment, she, too, glimpsed something more. Perhaps she saw the wonder of a crucified Christ.

Who Is This God?

Who is this God whose declaration of favor leads to the death of a firstborn son? Who is this God of promise and pain, who speaks of greatness then comes as a babe in a feeding trough? Who is he who sends a Messiah to die, and brings a mother to watch his death?

Who is this God?

He is the one who breaks us.

He is the one who remakes us ... at the foot of the cross.

I remember coming to grips with this breaking and remaking God one day after Sara's death. I was still grappling with our miscarriages, I'd lost a book contract, and our little home-church plant had died too. It seemed that everywhere I looked, I glimpsed death stalking. So I wondered and wrestled and asked, "What if ...? Why ...? Where was God in the face of all this death?"

Who was God?

That day I sat on a large boulder at the beach and watched the waves crash against the rocky shore. Beyond me the sun shone on the black water. It glinted then drowned in the dark expanse of waves. I turned back to the surf as it pounded against the rocks, splashed over them, glittered with myriad colors.

Who is this God? He is the one who breaks us. He is the one who remakes us ... at the foot of the cross.

A huge outcropping of jagged rock towered over the waves. Again and again the surf beat against it, throwing itself against the craggy surface, withdrawing, only to do it again. And again. And again.

With relentless persistence, the water broke against the rock. And still the rock didn't move. Only the water changed. Shattered. Molded to the shape of the stone.

I wrapped my arms around my knees and drew my legs close to my chest. I tried to pray but couldn't. I could only watch the waves against the rock. Watch them and feel their brokenness.

It's over. Done. Finished. The words whispered through my mind. And I knew they were true.

Our church plant was over. My book was dead. We had no more chances for another child. And I'd never see Sara's smiling face again.

I'd prayed, I'd hoped, I'd thrown myself against the mercy of God.

And still death came.

Just like that.

Yet, as I sat there, I found myself still crashing up against the immovable rock of God's will. All my tears, all my frustrations, all the disappointments, like dark, murky waves in my soul.

My gaze fell on the surf again. On the strange color of greenish black. It, too, was dark and ugly. Until it crashed against the rock.

I sat back and watched the water splash up in an arc of pure, clean white. Then it changed, reflecting a rainbow of color from the sunlight. And for that moment, it wasn't dark. It wasn't murky. It was stunningly beautiful. But only when it was broken on the rocks.

Paul quotes Isaiah 8:14 in Romans 9:33, saying, "As it is written: 'See, I lay in Zion a stone that causes people to stumble and a rock that makes them fall, and the one who believes in him will never be put to shame.'"

Jesus, who faced death for me, who died on the cross while his mother watched—he is my Rock. He is the one I fall upon, cast myself upon, just like the water throws itself against the craggy rocks.

And there, on the beach that day, I saw a glimmer of the truth. I am the surf. It is only when I am broken on Jesus that I reflect the light, shine with a rainbow of colors. It is then that I am able to be molded in his shape, just as the water molds to the shape of the stone when it falls back to the rock. Then the darkness is cleansed, the ugliness transformed, the water beautiful to behold.

Only God can do that. And he does it at the cross, in the moment when death seems to have its way.

Too many times I've heard people say to "just have faith." To them I think it means to never doubt, never struggle, never be broken. But as I sat there at the water's edge, I began to see that real faith, true faith, is the kind that casts itself against the rock. It's the kind that sits at the cross watching a son die and does not give up.

Death will break us. But we will become beautiful, will be transformed, will become who God has always dreamed we will be.

Death hurts, whether it's the death of a loved one, a dream, a job, a hope, or a promise. Death will break us. But in being broken, we will become beautiful. We will be transformed. We will become who God has always dreamed we will be.

Because faith—true faith—keeps coming back, despite the darkness, despite the hurt. Faith arcs up from brokenness. It clings to the Rock. It surrenders to the will of the immovable stone. And so it is transformed into a thing of wonder and beauty. Only in brokenness can it be filled with color and light.

And through the water, I see that it is the same for us.

Death is the doorway to becoming.

That place where dreams die, hopes come to naught, and promises all seem forgotten—there we are broken and remade. God changes everything for his glory.

In the impossible place, the impossible happens.

Wonder is born.

CHAPTER 15

A Shocking Transformation

Resurrection

LUKE 24:1 – 12

In a place where no one could see what was happening, everything changed. In the silence of a tomb, Jesus came to life. In the midst of darkness and despair, when hope was dead and buried, glory exploded into our world. Death was defeated, hope reborn.

The stone was rolled away to reveal a wonder greater and deeper than anyone could have imagined. More than Mary ever could have dreamed.

Jesus was alive.

And nothing would ever be the same again.

Death itself was transformed.

My heart catches at the thought. Could it be? Could it really be true? Because if it is, then every single hard and horrible thing in my life can also be transformed for God's glory. If it is true, nothing is impossible. Not anymore.

A wild hope. A breathtaking beauty.

In the midst of darkness, on a cold slab in a death-filled tomb ... Jesus rose from the dead.

In my dark tombs, all I know is the cold slab of fear, and I can't imagine anything good coming from this moment ... but Jesus lives.

Resurrection changes everything.

Resurrection changes everything.

Where was Mary that first Easter morning? Was she among the other women who went to the tomb to anoint Jesus' body with spices (Luke 24:10)? Luke doesn't list her, but she could have been there. Had she gone home to Galilee? Perhaps, but she was in John's care now. Or was she with the disciples, hidden away, not knowing what else could go wrong? We don't know. We do know that John was in charge of her care (John 19:26–27), and she was there among the disciples after Jesus' ascension (see Acts 1:14). So I believe it is likely she was there that morning with the disciples, waiting, trembling, praying, afraid of what else the Jews and Romans might do.

I believe she was there when the first rumors of resurrection changed the world.

Perhaps it happened something like this ...

Mary Tells Her Story

He is dead. Buried. And hope with him. I don't know what to believe anymore. I don't know what to think.

So I huddle here, in the first wisps of a breaking dawn. I shiver with my shawl tight around my shoulders. And I blink into the first ribbons of morning.

Why does the sun dare to shine? Why does the night not last forever?

Doesn't it know? He is dead.

I grip the folds of my dress in trembling fingers.

And I wait.

For what?

I couldn't sleep. How could I? But I'm not awake either. Not really. I exist in this in-between place. I cannot go forward. I cannot go back.

Because he's dead. The Messiah is dead. And I am all out of tears.

I am dead too.

Dead inside.

Broken.

He changed me, my Messiah-son. Once, I was a wide-eyed girl, eager to be the maidservant of my God. I loved, I trusted, I surrendered. And I had no idea. No idea what surrender would mean. No idea that God would destroy my every expectation, crush me, remake me, and lead me here.

Here to the spot where I cannot go forward. Cannot go back. Where I sit in the darkness of the dawning of a new day and wait for ... *what, Lord? What am I waiting for?*

You have changed me. He changed me. In the journey from a manger to a cross, I became more than a mother. I was Jesus' disciple. I still am. But who do I follow now? A dead son? A dead hope? A dead King?

Sunlight filters through the window, sickly at first. Then bright. I close my eyes, press a hand against the ache in my chest.

I don't weep. I only sit here in the waves of growing light.

I sit because I don't know what else to do. In my mind, I imagine Jesus there in the tomb. I see his shadow in the darkness. I see the fine linen cloth stained with his blood. And I turn my head away.

Some things hurt too much to be imagined.

A few of our women went to the tomb this morning. Went to anoint his dead body with spices, as is customary. I should have gone with them. But I couldn't. I just couldn't.

They will have to get someone to roll away the heavy stone. Then they will go in. And they will prepare his body.

They will do it well.

And I will sit here and wait for something, for nothing ... for a new day to dawn.

I tug at the ends of my shawl.

Something crashes downstairs. And I hear voices. High, panicked. Shrill. The women. What has happened at the tomb?

I race downstairs, stumble into the room. The men are there, the disciples. Peter, John, Matthew, Andrew, and the others. Their eyes are wide, their mouths open. And before them stand the women who had gone to the tomb.

How could they be back so soon?

The women are talking now, Mary of Magdala taking the lead. The story comes out in gasps, in short, panting spurts.

"He wasn't there."

Peter scowls. "What do you mean, 'He wasn't there'?"

"They have taken the Lord out of the tomb, and we don't know where they have put him!"

Joanna steps forward. "Mary! All we know is that Jesus was not there. The tomb ... he's not in the tomb!"

My heart sinks. Someone took his body. Could they not just leave him be, even in death?

John echoes my fears. "Are you sure you didn't see who took the body?"

Mary shakes her head. "You don't understand." Her voice softens. "I don't even understand."

Mary, the mother of James, glances at me. "No one took the body," she whispers.

Then Mary Magdalene looks straight at Peter. Her eyes pierce his. "We went to the tomb. We had our spices. We had our worries. We had our fears." She swallows. "We didn't know who would roll away the stone. But we needn't have been concerned. When we got there, the stone was rolled away already. So we went in."

Joanna touches Mary's arm. "And he wasn't there."

Mary nods. "His body was gone."

Peter crosses his arms. "The tomb was empty?"

Mary bites her lip. "Not exactly. But—but ... you'll never believe us." She shakes her head. Her shoulders straighten. "Men appeared, they came out of nowhere. And they were like no men we had ever seen."

Her words hit me, wash like a breaker into my soul. *Could it be?*

"Their clothes dazzled like lightning. And we—we fell down on our faces. We were so afraid."

Do not be afraid.... The words echo through my mind. And I see him again, my angel from so long ago. I see his gleaming clothes, his kind eyes, his stern jaw. I hear his words. "He will be great and will be called the Son of the Most High. The Lord God will give him the throne of his father David, and he will reign over Jacob's descendants forever; his kingdom will never end." Never end. So many promises, so many dreams.

An angel heralded my son's coming. And angels came at the end.

But could it be that this is not the end? The cross, the tomb, is not the end at all? "No word from God will ever fail," he told me.

And suddenly, I dare to hope.

Could it be?

For a moment, John turns his eyes toward me, and I know he is remembering, too, remembering my stories of a shining messenger from God speaking impossible words with impossible promises to a young girl in Galilee.

Did these tell impossible truths too?

John's eyes widen.

And the women speak again. Mary at first and then Joanna. "I know you don't believe us. I know it's hard to believe."

What did the angels say? What did they tell you? The words rush through my mind, but I cannot say them aloud. Not yet.

But the women answer anyway. "They said to us, 'Why do you look for the living among the dead? He is not here; he has risen!' Risen, Peter! Risen, John! He is risen! What does it mean?"

I steady myself, a hand against the wall. *Risen? Risen!* My heart thuds within me.

The men shake their heads. "What are you saying, women?" Thomas scowls. Andrew glares. "Crazy talk." They mutter, they grumble. They cross their arms. Turn away.

But the women don't stop. "The angels said more," Joanna whispers. Her voice grows deeper. "Remember how he told you, while he was still with you in Galilee: 'The Son of Man must be delivered over to the hands of sinners, be crucified and on the third day be raised again'? We remember."

I remember too. I remember all that, and more.

No word from God will ever fail....

The men don't turn back. But Peter does. And then John. Peter looks at the women, his face pale. John looks at me.

And then they run. Out the door. Down the path. Toward the tomb.

I follow.

But I cannot keep up. They run so fast. I see the puff of dust from sandaled feet. I hear the scrabble of small stones, taste the sharpness of the morning air.

And still they run. I run. Toward the tomb, toward hope, toward the impossible.

So here I am ... *running again*. Running toward him.

Suddenly I am glad. I want to run. Always, forever, running toward my Savior-son.

John reaches the tomb first. He stops at the entrance, touches the stone, rolled away just as the women had said.

Peter doesn't stop. He plunges inside.

I slow. Afraid, unafraid. Despairing, filled with hope.

John stares into the tomb. And then he, too, goes in.

Moments later they emerge. John turns. And they are changed. Changed!

Like men in a dream they walk toward me. As he passes, Peter whispers three words: "Could it be?"

They stagger back along the path, out of the garden.

This time, I do not follow them. Trembling, I approach the tomb, the place of death, despair ending. One step. Another. And then I am there. I run my fingers over the cold stone. I press my palm against the doorway.

Do I dare?

I step inside.

He is not here.

The strips of linen are lying there, as well as the cloth that had been wrapped around his head. The cloth is still lying in its place, separate from the linen. If someone stole the body, they'd have taken the grave clothes. No one would place the linens neatly to the side, folded ... just as I taught him to fold when he was a boy. The same corners, the same tuck ... could it be?

Could it be?

I stumble backward.

This, this changes everything.

I can barely grasp it. I turn away. Away from the tomb, away from death, away from despair.

I am like one coming back from death myself ... coming out of a tomb, coming out of the numbness of fear, of horror, and of sorrow.

And I know the truth. In my heart, I know it.

No word from God will ever fail. *He is risen!* He has taken death itself and defeated it. He is the Son of the Most High. His kingdom will never end.

He is risen. And all is new, different.

The sunlight stabs my eyes, and I welcome it. I lift my face to the warmth, soak in the dawning of a new day.

A new day, because he is risen, and I see.... He rose, but we have been resurrected, our lives forever changed. He is alive, but it is we who live because of him. Now everything can be changed, made new. Not just me but every single thing that sin has touched.

Nothing is beyond this power, this love that raised my son. That raised our Son.

So I see. He is more than I ever dreamed. He is more than I ever could have imagined. This son of mine is not only my Messiah, he is my God.

From this moment on, my whole life, our whole world, is transformed.

Resurrection Wonder

Is it true? Can God take the things that reek of death and misery and make them new? Can he raise not only his own Son but us as well? Can he transform tragedy into something of amazing glory?

He can.

He will.

He does.

The power of resurrection defeats the power of death. Jesus

makes it true. Not only in our physical deaths but also in all those places in our lives that seem horrible, hopeless, hard, and hurtful.

I know, because Jesus rose. And I know, because somehow God did the impossible for me. He changed death to new life. Twice.

A Son

Twenty years. Twenty years on the crazy journey through infertility and miscarriage. Twenty years of tracking cycles, taking tests, visiting doctors, watching, waiting, organizing my life around hoped-for babies that rarely came.

> *The power of resurrection defeats the power of death.... Not only in our physical deaths but also in all those places that seem horrible, hopeless, hard, and hurtful.*

Twenty years. Four final miscarriages, and I was done. It was over. All the frozen embryos were used up. The bank account was dry, and I had turned forty.

Forty.

I'd delivered bags of little clothes to the pregnancy center. I'd gotten rid of a closetful of baby things. All the little bibs were gone. No baby swings or strollers. No more bottles or booties. It was finished. I had closed the door on that portion of my life. I had rolled the stone over the entrance to the tomb and sealed it tight with tears and sorrow and the knowledge that the end had come in a way I never wanted, never hoped for, always prayed against.

And yet it was over.

The brother the girls had prayed for — over. The baby they'd begged God to give us — over. My hope for two more children — dead and in the tomb.

Many long months passed.

And then something odd occurred. My normally regular cycle was late. Weeks late. Did I have a tumor? Was menopause starting early? What had gone wrong?

I bought a pregnancy test. But I knew it would be negative. Of course it would be. Twenty years of not being able to get pregnant and have a baby without major medical intervention told me that there was no way I could be pregnant now, in my forties, with no help. But I had to at least take a test before calling my doctor to find out what was really wrong with me.

My husband was outside driving his tractor when I slipped into the bathroom and unwrapped a plain white stick. I followed the instructions then waited. Two minutes. Two tiny minutes to discover the impossible was somehow true.

I stared in disbelief as two lines appeared in the test window. Positive. Unbelievable.

Could it be?

I ran out to the yard and flagged Bryan down on his tractor. He shut off the engine.

"You aren't going to believe this." I waved the white test stick in his direction.

He took it from me. Stared. And like the disciples before him, shook his head. "That can't be right."

"I know."

"Call the doctor."

I did. She laughed at me. After twenty years of infertility, what else could she do but laugh? And seven and a half months later, right on time, we had a beautiful baby boy. A miracle baby who came from a tomb I thought sealed, who rose from a hope that had been dead. A boy born after I turned forty, my first child not conceived through extensive treatment.

God had brought his resurrection power into my life, and nothing would be the same again.

A Daughter

Then, two years later, the miracle repeated and a baby girl was born into our family—the last two children I had hoped for, prayed for, and known that all hope was dead for.

But Jesus rose from the dead.

And that changes everything.

Now, as I watch my preschooler learning to form his letters, as he practices writing "Mom" on a card filled with misshapen hearts, as he hands me yellow "fowlers" that others might call weeds, I remember that God is full of surprises, and purpose. As I kiss my baby girl and gaze into her wide, brown eyes, as she giggles and wipes her boogers across her cheek, as she throws her arms wide for a hug from Mommy, I hold her tight and can barely breathe for the wonder of it.

Does it always happen that way? No. Does God always give the barren woman a houseful of children? Does he always cure cancer? Does he always save prodigals? Does he always mend marriages?

No.

But he has risen from the dead. And that still changes everything. We can always have hope, because Jesus defeated our last enemy. He defeated death itself.

And so there is nothing — NOTHING — that cannot be transformed by his love, the same love, the same power, that raised Jesus from the grave.

Nothing is impossible. Nothing is hopeless. Nothing is beyond his reach.

Could it be?

Yes!

The Expert at Transforming

Mary knew it too.

Imagine her watching her son die. Imagine her knowing he'd been placed in the tomb. The horror, the misery, the unbelievable pain. Dead. Gone. Buried. She must have been thinking, *Nothing good could come of this. How could it?*

And yet it did.

Jesus. Was. Raised!

And that simple fact tells us that no matter how dark, no matter how horrible, God can transform. He can make new. We can always have hope ... because of the empty tomb. Because Jesus was raised from the dead. And this resurrection was not like that of Lazarus, Jairus's daughter, or the widow's son. He was not raised to die again; he was transformed. He was made new. He rose to real life, forever-life. As commentator David Garland says, "Jesus ... was not raised to resume his life on earth but to move to a new kind of bodily existence."

A new kind of life! Even Jesus was transformed. And in that moment, death was transformed too. "Where, O death, is your victory? Where, O death, is your sting?" asked Paul in 1 Corinthians 15:55.

But not only Jesus, not only death, but the disciples, too, were transformed. Something changed in them—forever. John Nolland says, "It can hardly be doubted that some powerful and life-transforming experience overtook the early disciples." They were changed by the resurrection. They, too, were made new. And through them, the whole world was changed. The resurrection changed their lives, their world, and all of history.

And Mary was a part of that. She was one of the disciples. And so are we.

The resurrection changes everything. It gives us a real, tangible hope. It makes our lives into a mission.

If there's one thing God is an expert at, it's transforming the horrible into the holy. It's making the worst into something of amazing beauty to reveal a wondrous God to a hurting world.

And we know it's true, because Jesus lives.

As it was for the disciples and Mary, when we encounter the risen Christ, even our worst nightmares can become the place of glory. Even the things that seem irredeemable can be saved. Because the power that raised Christ from the dead is available to us in our everyday, every-moment, ordinary, I-can't-believe-there's-hope-for-this situations.

We aren't taught to think that way, so resurrection is confusing at first. It was for the disciples, it must have been for Mary, and it is often for us as well.

Roll Away the Stone

Most of the disciples didn't even want to roll away the stone. They didn't want to go to the tomb at all. Only a few women went, only those who would be too weak to roll the stone from the tomb's entrance. Mark 16:3 tells us, "And they asked each other, 'Who will roll the stone away from the entrance of the tomb?'" Only those few women were brave enough to approach the grave. The others stayed far away, hidden, afraid.

> *To be the first to experience the power of the resurrection, sometimes we have to be brave enough to come to the tomb.*

To be the first to experience the power of the resurrection, sometimes we have to be brave enough to come to the tomb. We must face the very thing that represents the worst of our fears, the depths of our sorrow.

But how will we roll away the stone? How can we get past the barriers that separate us from Jesus? The women asked the same question. And they get the same answer: God himself will take care of that. He rolled away the stone. All they had to do was approach, come to him, even though they thought there was no hope and he was days dead.

That's all we have to do too. Come to the tomb. Come to the place where things seem impossible. And plan to meet Jesus there.

God will roll away the stone. He will reveal the truth.

An Empty Tomb and Grave Clothes

But you may not understand it. Not yet.

We see an empty tomb and think something worse is happening. We think, *Someone has stolen the body*. We expect more pain. But what is really happening is that God is on the move. He is bringing life, newness, wonder ... but we don't see him yet. All we see is the empty tomb. All we see are grave clothes.

And it is in those places in life—where we're trembling in fear, confused, wondering, expecting the worst, when we're thinking, *What else could go wrong?*—it is then that God is whispering to us, *Why do you look for the living among the dead? He is not here. He is risen!*

Risen!

And just as he said to the women, he says to us, *Remember what I told you?* In that moment, just as with the women, he is calling us to believe the truth even when we don't yet see him. He is calling us to live in the reality of resurrection, of hope, of knowing that God is the expert at transforming the worst things into glory. We can live from that truth even when all we see is emptiness and grave clothes.

Know that Jesus is risen. God is on the move.

Encounter the risen Christ and let your world be transformed. Forever.

Because Christ is raised ...

> *Therefore, my dear brothers and sisters, stand firm. Let nothing move you. Always give yourselves fully to the work of the Lord, because you know that your labor in the Lord is not in vain. (1 Cor. 15:58)*

Who Is This God?

So who is this God who rose from the dead never to die again? Who is he who transformed death itself? Who is he who calls us to live in the wonder of resurrection and see our world transformed?

He is the God who makes all things new.

He is the God who transformed my infertility, the God who transformed my pain. And he can transform yours. Because that's what he does. That's who he is.

He is the God who transformed the cross. And if he can do it for two rough-hewn pieces of wood, he can do it for you as well.

Consider the symbol of the cross. In Mary's day, it represented horror and death, the worst kind of execution. To the ancient Roman world, it was a symbol of everything awful, bad, terrifying. It was ugly. It meant disgust and destruction. It meant shame and agony and loss. To see a cross was to see a symbol of the worst kind of death possible.

That's what the cross was ... until Christ transformed it.

Right now, in my jewelry box, I have several sets of cross earrings and necklaces. I don't wear them to let people know I'm a Christian, I wear them as a reminder of God's power to transform. The cross is a perfect picture of how God transforms the ugly into the beautiful. I wouldn't wear a hangman's noose or a guillotine or a gilded electric chair. But I do wear crosses. Why? Because God has *transformed* the cross.

We use it to decorate our homes. We put it in the front of our churches. It has become a symbol recognized all over the world. And it doesn't mean death and shame anymore. It means life, salvation, redemption, love, and hope.

The cross is where death turned to life, where joy triumphed over sorrow, where my life was redeemed. The cross, once nothing more than an executioner's tool, is now a symbol of God's redeeming love. It has become the thing that symbolizes everything that matters to us. It means new life.

And that is a shocking transformation.

If God can do that for the cross, he can do it for you. And he will. He can take the awful things in your life and transform them, too, for his glory. Romans 8:28 says, "God works for the good of those who love him, who have been called according to his purpose." It doesn't say that all things that happen are good but that God can turn the hard things into good. He can make them into a shining testimony of his love and faithfulness.

But if they are going to be transformed, you must take those difficult, sometimes painful experiences, and offer them to God. You need to come to the tomb, even if you come with trembling, even if you come with tears.

Or will you be like Judas, who died in despair when forgiveness and new life were just days away? Will you hang from the end of a rope, or will you come to the tomb, trembling? Because we've all betrayed him.

Or will you be like the chief priests and elders, who made up their own story to bury the truth (see Matt. 28:11–15)? Will you live a lie, or will you come to the tomb and believe?

The cross, once nothing more than an executioner's tool, is now a symbol of God's redeeming love.

Will you be like the soldiers who saw and ran away? For money they hid what they knew to be true and spread rumors instead (see Matt. 28:11–15). Will you face the strange, the uncertain, the mystery of the tomb ... or will you cover over the truth with false platitudes, even if they are ones of God's "goodness"?

Will you, afraid, confused, doubting, approach the gravesite, peek inside, and be changed forever? Will you be Jesus' follower, the one who approaches the tomb with spices in her hands?

Come, believe that what Jesus did for the cross he will do for you. The worst things in your life can be transformed into life and beauty. Hear the whisper of angels, "Why do you look for the living among the dead? ... He has risen!" And you are raised with him. So even at the tombs of life, God is calling you to live with expectant joy, knowing that he is not dead. Even if you can't see him, he is on the move; he is working.

Because now, anything, everything, can be transformed by his love.

Let him roll away the stone.

CHAPTER 16

The Wonder of His Love

Pentecost

ACTS 1:14

So we come back to the beginning, to the question of love on a laundry room floor. To the question of who we are, who I am, to this God who sends a gift so amazing, so divine, that there has never been anything like it.

"Show me the wonders of your great love," the psalmist said to God (17:7). And in the first chapters of Acts, we see that wonder. We see love.

We see it in tongues of fire. In dozens of languages spoken by simple, uneducated followers of Christ. We see it in a gift beyond any other, received as the disciples pray and call on an ascended God.

And we see it in a moment in Mary's life that is like her first encounter with God but so unlike it too. So much more.

More wonder.

More beauty.

More love.

Just as before, angels announce Jesus' future coming. Just as then, Mary submits, prays, waits. However, now she prays not alone but with others, with those who are the first in the body of Christ. And again, the Spirit comes on her. On them.

But this time there is no baby, no rounding belly, no startled husband-to-be. This time the Spirit comes. The Spirit remains. And God is again in her. But now he is here to stay. With them all.

God gives his gift of the Spirit to Mary, to the disciples, to all who trust in Christ as Savior and Lord. A gift that means all the promises have come true. A gift that means we are not alone. Love has come to be with us, to live in us.

Then. Now. Forever.

What does it mean to live in a love like that? What does it mean to know, to truly know in the depths of your being, that God's Spirit is in you, that he loves you and will not abandon you or forsake you? He has come to stay because you are highly favored. You are most blessed.

You are not Esau. You are not Cain.

You are Mary, receiver of the Spirit of God.

For Mary it may have happened something like this:

Mary Tells Her Story

I've seen him. I've touched him with my hands, held him in my arms. He was beautiful, this risen Savior of mine. He appeared before us not once but many times. He ate, he laughed, he taught. And I thought I couldn't be happier. I couldn't be more full of joy.

I was wrong.

There was more to come.

I felt the scars on his hands. I saw the puckering of flesh on his feet. And I knew what he had done for us. He will carry those scars forever. For me.

I remembered the first time he came to me. We were eating

a simple meal of bread and fish. John was chiding Peter, saying that he must have thrown the net on the wrong side of the boat. Andrew laughed. Philip snickered.

And then he was there. My Jesus.

He was laughing too. His eyes alight, his cheeks rosy, his teeth flashing in the candlelight. And I was reminded of the boy who used to run through my kitchen, laughing, with a gift of wildflowers in his hand.

His hands hold a different gift now. The gift of forgiveness, of freedom, of a hope that I can only barely grasp.

He sat beside Peter and broke a piece of bread from Peter's loaf. "In remembrance of me," he whispered.

And then his gaze fell on me.

"Will you pass the fish?"

"I hope you washed before coming to eat."

He grinned. And in that moment, all my doubts fled. I knew who I was. Highly favored. Blessed. Not because I was mother of the Messiah but because I was the disciple of my forever King. I was his. I always would be. And I wanted him to stay with me forever.

But my Jesus never would be the Messiah I wanted him to be.

Again, he surprised me. I was there that day in Bethany, and I watched him ascend into the clouds. He left me alone. Again. He left to a place I could not follow. Not yet.

And then the angels appeared. Always the angels. "Men of Galilee," they said to us, "why do you stand here looking into the sky? This same Jesus, who has been taken from you into heaven, will come back in the same way you have seen him go into heaven."

He will come again.

I smile and remember another thing he said to us—to wait in Jerusalem for the promise of the Father.

So I wait. I pray. And I am at peace.

The God who raised Jesus from the dead will do as he said. The gift will come.

We all know it's true. And so we wait here, in one accord, in the upper room. Together. We pray and we eat. We praise and we remember.

I have waited before. But this is a different kind of waiting. This is waiting filled with hope, full of joy. So I wait for the promise and relish the peace in this waiting.

Waiting for the Spirit.

We are telling each other stories of his ministry when it happens. We are talking of the wind on the waters of the sea when another wind comes. Comes through the open window and ruffles the hem of my garment. It grows into a sound like a mighty rushing. And the wind, the rushing, the roar fills the entire house where we are sitting. Long strands of hair whip around my face. I taste the freshness of the wind and raise my hands to welcome it, this roaring breeze, this *pneuma*.

Light like deep orange fire appears above us. It writhes and bursts into a dozen tongues of flame. One rests on Peter, on Andrew, on John ... on everyone.

And then the fire comes on me.

And I know the Spirit in the fire. I have felt him before.

But this is unlike a robe coming on me. Unlike a force settling on my shoulders, settling in my womb.

This time, every part of me is filled. Filled with a wonder like I have never known. Filled with joy. Filled with love.

Filled. Forever. And from this moment, I know that I am not alone. I am not abandoned. I am his beloved. I am his precious one. I am cherished. Forever.

Because he has given me the gift of his Spirit.

He has sent me indwelling love.

The Wonders of His Great Love

The last time we see Mary in the New Testament, she is with the disciples in prayer (Acts 1:14). She is waiting for a promise. She is waiting in faith.

I find that encouraging somehow—that this one who had been through so much; who surrendered, expected, dealt with disappointments and fear; who thought her son was crazy; who watched him die ... in the end is on her knees, in the body of Christ, waiting for a gift she knows will come.

> *The last time we see Mary in the New Testament, she is with the disciples in prayer. She is waiting for a promise.*

We find a woman who knows how to wait, how to trust, how to be a disciple among disciples. A blessed woman, favored, not because life has turned out the way she hoped and dreamed but because it has not.

Because God had his way. In her.

Looking Back on My Journey

So, as I look back on my life so far, I see a journey I never would have expected, a path that was not a part of my dreams.

I dreamed of three children. God dreamed of six. His dream was better. Harder, but better.

I dreamed of doing big, important things for God. I wanted to plant a church that brought thousands to Christ. I wanted to change a city for him. Or perhaps be a missionary or go to the inner city or do something that would somehow matter. But he dreamed of remaking me into the image of his Son. My "big things" weren't his masterpiece at all—*I* am. I am the big, important thing to him. And because I am changed, I can do the works that he has already prepared in advance for me to do (see Eph. 2:10). The important thing was never my "big things" but *me*. The rest will come because *I* am his masterpiece. *I* matter. His dream is better. Harder, but better.

Twenty years on the journey through infertility was hard. Six miscarriages were even harder. I wept over failed ministries and lost hopes. I cried out to God, thought he had lost his mind. And I pounded my fists against a laundry room floor, and the washer sloshed, and I knew, just knew, that God didn't love me.

I was wrong.

And God showed me how wrong I was not by suddenly doing everything I'd wanted, everything I'd hoped for. Nothing in my circumstances changed that morning. But I changed. Because God showed me that I was not Esau, I was not Cain.

I was Mary.

Favored. Blessed. And living a life that he'd chosen for me, even if I had not. He had sent me his Spirit. And I was loved.

I know that now, because I have discovered him through Mary's journey ... and through my own.

So would I go back? Would I change it all? Maybe. In my perfect world, there wouldn't be infertility, there wouldn't be miscarriage or divorce or the death of loved ones or failure in ministry.

But this isn't a perfect world. And blessedness is in the journey. It is in the running. Running to Egypt when you don't want to go but you know he is sending you. Running to Jerusalem because you believe he is lost, but in truth, he is waiting for you. Running to the cross because he is dying for you there. Running to the tomb, and it is empty because, behold, he has made all things new. He has made you new.

So, no, I would not change it now. Because I see, I believe, that every step on this strange and wonder-filled journey is used by God not to make the world perfect but to perfect me, to make me like the Risen One, to make me who God created me to be. Nothing is wasted. Nothing is beyond his transforming touch.

Even barrenness, even death, even failure he has made new. He has taken them all, reformed them, resurrected them, to give me a hope beyond all hope, to fulfill his promises in ways I never could have dreamed.

Yet I still struggle. I still wonder. I still doubt.

Looking Back on Mary's Journey

So I look to Mary. I want to be like her, waiting, praying, trusting, a disciple among disciples, ready for the Spirit to move. I want to get up from the laundry room floor and say, "I am not alone. He is coming. I know he is coming for me. For us." I want to be able to trust even when nothing has gone as I hoped, as I dreamed, as I expected.

So again, I come to Mary's life walking on tiptoe, knowing I am treading where angels have trod. And I see again, she really wasn't so different from you and me. She had similar hopes, similar dreams.

She was just a young girl from the backwoods of Galilee. A girl with a plan and a heart.

It was a good plan, a good heart.

But the two could not exist together. Because her God, our God, has dreams of his own. Like you and me, Mary was called to more. Her God is our God. And I pray that we can encounter him again, afresh, anew.

I pray that we will live every day, every moment, in the knowledge that we are blessed, we are favored, we are deeply loved.

Like Mary.

So I think back to that young girl whose life was interrupted one day in Galilee.

I remember a girl who surrendered to God and then saw her life turn out nothing like she expected, a girl who would face the most horrific kind of pain imaginable, a woman who would be called favored and most blessed. Mary, who …

- would be scorned by her village
- would take a long trip while nine months pregnant

- would give birth to her firstborn son in a barn
- would have to flee to a foreign country when that boy was a toddler because a king wanted him dead
- would search three days for her lost son, who then would not even apologize for making her panic
- would think her son had lost his mind
- would see him arrested, beaten, and hung on a Roman cross
- would see her Messiah-son die right in front of her eyes

And every expectation would be broken, every hope shattered, every dream killed.

All the promises were fulfilled ... in ways Mary never could have expected.

But Mary would also see her son rise again. And she would become who she was created to be — the mother of the Savior of us all.

And all the promises were fulfilled ... in ways she never could have expected.

All the hopes were reborn ... out of the empty tomb.

All the dreams came true in ways even deeper, more wondrous, than she, or we, ever could have dared to imagine.

Mary in Acts

Mary saw Jesus risen, knew beyond a doubt that he was alive. She could now stop striving, stop worrying, stop fretting that somehow God would fail her. Instead, she learned to wait and to trust. And as we will see, she learned to tell of God's unexpected wonder because she was filled with the guarantee of forever. She was filled with the very Spirit of God himself. She became his own.

Lloyd John Ogilvie says, "The Holy Spirit is the immanent and intimate approach to man of the living God whom we know through Jesus Christ." God himself, the one of whom John writes,

"God is love" (1 John 4:8), takes up his dwelling place deep in our very own souls. Perfect love comes to live intimately in you and me.

"Mary is present only here in Acts, as she was present at the beginning of the Gospel, and in both cases she is associated with a special work of the Holy Spirit. Just as she was overshadowed by the Spirit, so shall, in a different sense, all Jesus' faithful followers be," says scholar Ben Witherington III. And that is the essence of love. True love. Real love. The love we all long for. The love I could not fathom from the laundry room floor.

Beyond Acts

Mary knew God's love. So did the disciples. They were filled with it. And yet none of them would go on to live a life free from more grief, pain, or death. Not even Mary. Instead, she would see the execution of more sons. Jesus' brother James would be condemned by the Sanhedrin and stoned to death around the year AD 66. We don't know how his other brothers died, but we know the early church was persecuted. We know Christians were stoned, sent to the lions' den, crucified, beaten, and driven from their homes. We know that Mary's life didn't suddenly become easy.

But it was filled with a love unlike anything she had experienced before because the Spirit had come to live in her, to live in all who followed Jesus. They were filled with a Love that not only died and rose again but that found a way to be with believers forever. A Love that sent his Spirit so that we would no longer be alone. We are a part of the one who is love himself. We are his bride, his beloved, his treasure.

That is what it means to be highly favored. That is what it is to be most blessed.

Ogilvie describes it this way:

My experience of the Holy Spirit has been like a drumbeat. When I met Christ and turned my life over to him, inviting him to live his life in me, the drumbeat began—softly at first, then persistently, indefatigably. The rhythms have never ceased. This is no distant drummer. The indwelling Lord has sounded the cadences of a living pulsebeat from within my soul.... The drumbeat of the Master is love—his love for me, and through me to others.

The drumbeat of the Spirit is love. If you ask him, he will beat in your heart.

Perfect Love came to make his home in Mary, in you, in me. Through him we can discover the depth of God's wondrous, forever love in our lives. We can delve deep into the meaning of that love until we are changed by it. We can know that everything, even the most difficult things, can become means to experience God's love in our lives, to draw us nearer to him, to grow deep.

So, I wrestle with the wonder of living in the reality of God's love every day, every moment. I wrestle to know this love that surpasses knowledge. I wrestle to know him. Because in knowing who he is, I will discover who I am. I will live as one favored, highly blessed. I will live as one loved to the cross, and back.

Because the Promised One has come, because he has given his Spirit, and because I am made new by him, I am not who I used to be.

I know I am loved.

Who Are You?

So, who are you in this life where things don't go as expected, where dreams die, where hope trembles, where the Messiah is crucified while his mother watches, helpless? Who are you when life looks nothing like you thought it would, when fears whisper, when you wonder, *Does God really love me?*

You Are the Pearl

Listen to this familiar parable again: "Again, the kingdom of heaven is like a merchant looking for fine pearls. When he found one of great value, he went away and sold everything he had and bought it" (Matt. 13:45–46).

The kingdom of heaven is like a merchant. God is the merchant. He is the one searching for what is most precious to him. And when he finds it, he gives everything he has to make it his own.

You are the pearl of great price. He is searching for you. He gave everything for you. He gave his very life, so that you could receive the Spirit and belong to him forever. You are that precious. You are that cherished and wanted and loved. You are not only God's masterpiece, you are his treasure.

And nothing changes that. Not what anyone else says or does. Not losing a job, divorce, rejection, loss, friendship gone awry.... There is no one God loves more than you.

You Are Cinderella

You are Cinderella—and the shoe fits. You may still be dressed in your ratty, old work clothes with a handkerchief in your hair. You may still have a wicked stepmother and two mean stepsisters. You may still have an ugly cat and a tough day job. Everything may seem as it was before ... but it's all changed because the shoe fits and the Prince loves you. You are his.

He has chosen you. He died and rose again to transform you. He sent his Spirit so you can be his forever. The Spirit is the ring that guarantees the promise that weds you to him.

The injustices you've suffered fade. The hard times, the losses, the smudges on your face, the tears you've cried—they may still be there, but things are different now. You are the princess, you are loved, and that changes everything.

You Are Mary

The angel, the messenger, has come, and you are called by God to surrender to his dreams, his plans. You are called to an impossible life of privilege and pain, of favor and blessedness that will defy your every expectation. You are called by a God who loves you and created you for this.

What you've done before — your accomplishments and failures — don't matter now. You are chosen. You are favored. You are blessed.

You matter …

> when things go wrong,
> when life is crazy,
> when nothing makes sense,
> when you don't know how you're going
> to get through another day.

You are loved.

God is always seeking you, always calling you. Always whispering to you about the wonder of his love.

He has offered you his Spirit. The question is — do you hear him, do you see him, do you know he's there?

Will you kneel with Mary, with the disciples, and say, "I am the Lord's handmaiden, may it be to me as you have said"?

If you do, you will encounter Christ more deeply, more fully, with more wonder than you have ever dreamed.

What you've done before doesn't matter now. You are chosen. You are favored. You are blessed.

Will you be fully his? Will you let go? Will you embark on this wild ride with a God who loves you, who died for you, who rose again so you could be his masterpiece, so you could be his beloved?

Will you wait?

Will you trust?

Will you be filled?

Because that is what it means to be blessed and highly favored, in all the ups and downs and crazy turns of life.

Go, live every day, every moment, out of the fullness, the beauty, the wonder of that love …

> *For this reason I kneel before the Father, from whom every family in heaven and on earth derives its name. I pray that out of his glorious riches he may strengthen you with power through his Spirit in your inner being, so that Christ may dwell in your hearts through faith. And I pray that you, being rooted and established in love, may have power, together with all the Lord's holy people, to grasp how wide and long and high and deep is the love of Christ, and to know this love that surpasses knowledge — that you may be filled to the measure of all the fullness of God. (Eph. 3:14–19)*

CHAPTER 17

Eyewitness and Servant
Mary Tells Her Story

LUKE 1:2

L uke opens his gospel with these words:

> *Many have undertaken to draw up an account of the things that have been fulfilled among us, just as they were handed down to us by those who from the first were eyewitnesses and servants of the word. With this in mind, since I myself have carefully investigated everything from the beginning, I too decided to write an orderly account for you, most excellent Theophilus, so that you may know the certainty of the things you have been taught. (Luke 1:1–4)*

Then he goes on to tell us details of Mary's journey that only she could have told him. I believe that when he says "eyewitnesses and servants," Mary is included among them. When he says, "carefully investigated," I believe that means he interviewed Mary as well. She told her story.

She lived it, she was changed by it, and then she shared her journey so that all generations would call her blessed. Blessed because of who she saw God to be, blessed through the journey itself.

Through Mary's journey, we see God himself. In encountering him, how can we, too, not be changed, not be filled?

So even though we do not see Mary again after Acts 1:14, we do see her stories. We see her transformation from girl to mother, from mother to disciple, from disciple to one who waits, trusts, and is filled with the Spirit.

Through Mary's journey, we see God himself. And in encountering him, how can we, too, not be changed, not be filled?

I think it may have happened something like this. Come, travel with Mary one more time. Hear her heart, see her God....

Mary Tells Her Story

I sit here mending the thong of my sandal. My fingers work slowly now. My hands tremble. I sit and I watch and I wait.

Children play on the road before me. They giggle and scamper. They call out, but not to me. I smile as I listen.

Dust billows from the road. I see a young man cresting the hill. He lifts a hand in greeting, adjusts the pouch over his shoulder.

I squint to see him better; my eyes have grown weak over the long years. But my memory is sharp still. I remember everything. Everything.

And this doctor, this one they call Luke, says he wants to hear me. Wants me to tell him what I know of my son, my Messiah ... my God.

He strolls toward me, tousles the hair of one of the boys, picks up the ball they play with, throws it to the smallest boy. They laugh. And then the doctor comes to me.

He bows, and I pat the space beside me.

"I am making a careful study," he says. "Investigating everything about Jesus."

I raise my eyebrows. "Everything?" How can he investigate everything? There is so much, so much more than I ever dreamed possible.

He grins. "Perhaps not everything. But enough."

"Enough for what?"

"That they might see him. That even the Gentiles might know the truth and believe."

I nod. The whole world is changing because of him, because of my son, God's Son. His followers are persecuted, but they do not give up. Those who claim his name are killed, but still they claim him. They have fled, they have been flogged, they have died. And still they proclaim what he taught them.

So I will too.

I will tell it truthfully, painfully, honestly. I will tell of a God who revealed himself to me as a baby born in a barn, as a boy in the temple, as a Messiah who would not be who I thought he should be. I will tell of a journey to the cross and beyond it. I will tell a story of transformation, of hope, of wonder....

The Wonder of Your Story

I will tell my story too. Will you? God has asked me to tell my story all over the world, to talk of a God who took me on a journey I never wanted to go on, a God who wooed me through the pain of infertility, the brokenness of miscarriage, the sorrow of loss and failure. I've told the truth and wept in the telling, because my God is not a God of the struggle-free path. He rarely does what I want.

And still he calls me to testify, to witness to his strange, unexpected wonder. He tells me to speak honestly about my pain and give no easy answers. He calls me to wrestle ... always to wrestle.

And so I am glad that Mary wrestled, too, and when she told her story, it wasn't a pretty, polished picture of God's goodness. She didn't change the barn to a palace. She didn't explain away a boy who stayed behind in Jerusalem. She didn't make excuses for a Messiah who would not come out and be who she wanted him to be.

Nor did she tell of her doubt-free faith, of going from victory to victory, or give lofty explanations for those moments when life went awry. Instead, she spoke of struggle, of confusion, of darkness and times when nothing made sense. She told the truth of what life with her God was really like.

And by doing so, she has given me hope. Real hope. True hope.

And a mission. Because I am an eyewitness too. And so are you. I am his servant. I have experienced his strange, unexpected grace. I have walked the mountaintops and valleys with him.

My mission, and yours, is to tell the truth about our life with God, in all its messiness, with all its doubts, in all its imperfections. We must tell of a God of wonder who shatters our dreams and offers his own, who calls us to suffer and be transformed. We must speak of a God of wonder who breaks us and remakes us, a God we often don't understand but who still walks with us. A God who takes us to the cross, into the darkness, and to the tomb. A God who loves us in spite of it all.

Wrestle with the wonder of the living God.

Tell of the real Jesus, who died on that cross so that we might be made new. Tell of fear and hurt, wonder and transformation. Tell it starkly, truthfully.

Tell your story. Find the real God in it.

And wrestle.

Wrestle with the wonder of the living God. Breathtaking. Vibrant. And so often nothing like we expected him to be.

So wrestle.

And remember.

And tell of his breathtaking wonder.

Now enter, one final time, into the journey of the one called highly favored, blessed, chosen ...

Mary's Final Words

He settles beside me, this doctor-turned-disciple, with his stylus in his hand.

I close my eyes, and I prepare to encounter my God again in the story I will tell to Luke, to the world, to the generations upon generations to come.

So I begin. I start on an ordinary day, in an ordinary life, in an ordinary village tucked into the back corners of a region far from the hub of importance. I start with a girl and an angel and an impossible promise. And I tell how the promise came true.

I tell my story. And in telling it, I see that it's really not about me at all. It's about him. It always has been. Mine is not a story of amazing faith; it's a story of an amazing God. A God who led me on a journey I never expected. A God who took me deeper even than my dreams.

I talk, I tell, I remember. And I pray that you hear not my story but his. God's amazing story lived out in my life, in his life, and in yours.

Because Messiah came. He shattered every expectation and fulfilled every promise. He broke me, and he remade me. He transformed me, and I was made new. Every moment, every tear, every fear ... was worth it. Because I see ... I see *him*.

And he is more than I ever dared to dream.

So I ask, will you take this journey too? Will you run with a Messiah who is beyond your wildest imaginings? Will you embrace this God of breathtaking wonder?

Do you dare?

Author Note

Dear Fellow Traveler,

As I finish this story of Mary and her crazy, wondrous God, I glance out the window here at Starbucks and see an old man hunched over, sweeping up dried leaves in the parking lot. He sweeps one, then moves to another, gathering up dried remnants of life and hope. And as he sweeps the last leaves, I think back on this journey through Mary's life and wonder if there are leaves I should have gathered or leaves I should have left. Did I say enough? Did I say too much? Did you get a glimpse of the God that I see in Mary's life, and in my own? Did you see him in new ways in yours?

I hope so. I pray so. I pray that you've wrestled and wondered and encountered God in new and deeper ways—and that you've been transformed through the journey.

I pray that you find him in your own barns and at your tombs. I pray that you catch your breath at the wonder of God's love for *you*.

Thank you for taking this journey with me through Mary's life, and through mine. If you'd like to know more about me or my other books, please visit my website at VividGod.com and sign up for my newsletter, or join me for thoughts on finding the wonder of God in everyday life on Twitter (www.twitter.com/Marlo Schalesky) or Facebook (www.facebook.com/MarloSchalesky). I hope to hear from you!

> May God fill your life with
> his breathtaking wonder,
> Marlo

Sources

Introduction

13: *"Jacob I loved":* Romans 9:13.

Chapter 1

26: *"For all indicators":* R. Kent Hughes, *Luke (Vol. 1): That You May Know the Truth,* Preaching the Word (Wheaton, IL.: Crossway, 1998), 30.

28: *Green:* Joel B. Green, *The Gospel of Luke* (Grand Rapids: Eerdmans, 1997), 86.

28: *Origen:* Origen, quoted in Arthur A. Just Jr., ed., *New Testament, No. 3: Luke.* Ancient Christian Commentary on Scripture (Downers Grove, IL: InterVarsity, 2003), 14.

29: *Hughes:* Hughes, *Luke,* 34.

Chapter 2

43: *Prudentius:* Prudentius, *The Divinity of Christ,* 585–93, quoted in Arthur A. Just Jr., ed., *New Testament, No. 3: Luke.* Ancient Christian Commentary on Scripture (Downers Grove, IL: InterVarsity, 2003), 22.

43: *Hughes:* R. Kent Hughes, *Luke (Vol. 1): That You May Know the Truth,* Preaching the Word (Wheaton, IL.: Crossway, 1998), 42.

45: *Garland:* David E. Garland, *Luke,* Exegetical Commentary on the New Testament (Grand Rapids: Zondervan, 2011), 87.

45: *Garland:* Ibid., 90.

48: *"Blessed are you when you're rejected.":* See Luke 6:20–22.

Chapter 3

57: *Bock:* Darrell L. Bock, *Luke, Volume 1, 1:1–9:50,* Baker Exegetical Commentary on the New Testament (Grand Rapids: Baker, 1994), 209.

Chapter 4

66: *Jerome:* Jerome, quoted in Arthur A. Just Jr., ed., *New Testament, No. 3: Luke*, Ancient Christian Commentary on Scripture (Downers Grove, IL: InterVarsity, 2003), 39.

68: *Nolland:* John Nolland, *Luke 1–9:20*, Word Biblical Commentary, vol. 35A (Dallas: Word, 1989), 105.

68: *Craddock:* Fred B. Craddock, *Luke: Interpretation: A Bible Commentary for Teaching and Preaching* (Louisville: John Knox, 1990), 35.

71: *Hughes:* R. Kent Hughes, *Luke (Vol. 1): That You May Know the Truth*, Preaching the Word (Wheaton, IL.: Crossway, 1998), 83.

Chapter 5

76: *"Will the wild ox …?":* Job 39:9.

78: *"The ox knows its master":* Isaiah 1:3.

83: *Garland:* David E. Garland, *Luke*, Exegetical Commentary on the New Testament (Grand Rapids: Zondervan, 2011), 122.

83: *Francis:* St. Francis of Assisi, quoted in *The Liturgy of the Hours, Vol. 4* (Totowa, NJ: Catholic Book Publishing Co., 1975), 1465.

83: *Bede:* Bede, quoted in Arthur A. Just Jr., ed., *New Testament, No. 3: Luke*, Ancient Christian Commentary on Scripture (Downers Grove, IL: InterVarsity, 2003), 38.

84: *Garland:* Garland, *Luke*, 124.

87: *From the Ikos:* Quoted in Just, *New Testament, No. 3: Luke*, 37.

Chapter 6

95: *Craddock:* Fred B. Craddock, *Luke: Interpretation: A Bible Commentary for Teaching and Preaching* (Louisville: John Knox, 1990), 38.

96: *Larson:* Bruce Larson, *Luke*, The Communicator's Commentary (Waco, TX: W, 1983), 59.

97: *McKnight:* Scot McKnight, *The Real Mary* (Brewster, MA: Paraclete, 2007), 47–48.

Chapter 7

110: *Keener:* Craig S. Keener, *The Gospel of Matthew, A Socio-Rhetorical Commentary* (Grand Rapids: Eerdmans, 2009), 109.

112: *Osborne:* Grant R. Osborne, *Matthew*, Exegetical Commentary on the New Testament (Grand Rapids: Zondervan, 2010), 104–5.

117: *Chrysostom:* John Chrysostom, quoted in Manlio Simonetti, ed., *New Testament, No. 1a: Matthew 1–13*, Ancient Christian Commentary on Scripture (Downers Grove, IL: InterVarsity, 2001), 31.

Chapter 8

130: *Nolland:* John Nolland, *Luke 1–9:20*, Word Biblical Commentary, vol. 35A (Dallas: Word, 1989), 134.

130: *Hughes:* R. Kent Hughes, *Luke (Vol. 1): That You May Know the Truth*, Preaching the Word (Wheaton, IL.: Crossway, 1998), 102.

132: *Wilcock:* Michael Wilcock, *The Message of Luke: The Saviour of the World* (Downers Grove, IL: InterVarsity, 1979), 49.

132: *McKnight:* Scot McKnight, *The Real Mary* (Brewster, MA: Paraclete, 2007), 57.

133: *Hughes:* Hughes, *Luke*, 103.

133: *Nolland:* Nolland, *Luke 1–9:20*, 133.

Chapter 9

141: *"Let the light of your face":* Psalm 4:6–7.

141: *"Go, eat your food":* Ecclesiastes 9:7.

149: *Kostenberger:* Andreas J. Kostenberger, *John, Baker Exegetical Commentary of the New Testament* (Grand Rapids: Baker, 2004), 92.

149: *McKnight:* Scot McKnight, *The Real Mary* (Brewster, MA: Paraclete, 2007), 65.

150: *Burge:* Gary Burge, *John*, The NIV Application Commentary (Grand Rapids: Zondervan, 2000), 91.

151: *Carson:* D. A. Carson, *The Gospel according to John*, Pillar New Testament Commentary (Grand Rapids: Eerdmans, 1991), 171.

152: *Burge:* Burge, *John*, 104.

153: *Burge:* Ibid., 91.

Chapter 10

164: *McKnight:* Scot McKnight, *The Real Mary* (Brewster, MA: Paraclete, 2007), 75.

164: *McKnight:* Ibid., 77.

165: *Nolland:* John Nolland, *Luke 1–9:20,* Word Biblical Commentary, vol. 35A (Dallas: Word, 1989), 75.

Chapter 11

186: *Lewis:* C. S. Lewis, *The Problem of Pain* (1952; New York: HarperOne, 2009).

Chapter 12

198: *Carson:* D. A. Carson, *The Gospel according to John,* Pillar New Testament Commentary (Grand Rapids: Eerdmans, 1991), 616–17.

Chapter 13

206: *"In that day,' declares the Sovereign LORD":* Amos 8:9–10.

212: *Nolland:* John Nolland, *Luke 18:35–24:53,* Word Biblical Commentary, vol. 35C (Dallas: Word, 1989), 1160.

212: *Garland:* David E. Garland, *Luke,* Exegetical Commentary on the New Testament (Grand Rapids: Zondervan, 2011), 928.

Chapter 14

226: *Hughes:* R. Kent Hughes, *Luke (Vol. 2): That You May Know the Truth,* Preaching the Word (Wheaton, IL: Crossway, 1998), 395.

Chapter 15

243: *Garland:* David E. Garland, *Luke,* Exegetical Commentary on the New Testament (Grand Rapids: Zondervan, 2011), 944.

243: *Nolland:* John Nolland, *Luke 18:35–24:53,* Word Biblical Commentary, vol. 35C (Dallas: Word, 1989), 1182.

Chapter 16

255: *Ogilvie:* Lloyd John Ogilvie, *Drumbeat of Love* (Waco, TX: Word, 1976), 15.

256: *Witherington:* Ben Witherington III, *The Acts of the Apostles,* A Socio-Rhetorical Commentary (Grand Rapids: Eerdmans, 1998), 113–14.

256: *Ogilvie:* Ogilvie, *Drumbeat of Love,* 9.